The Gerald Coke Library. K.E.S.W

Britain and the Korean War

W0009855

KING EDWARD'S SCHOOL

* / 0 0 0 7 3 5 4 *

Making Contemporary Britain

General Editor: Anthony Seldon
Consultant Editor: Peter Hennessy

Institute of Contemporary British History
34 Tavistock Square, London WC1H 9EZ

Britain and the Korean War

Callum MacDonald

Basil Blackwell

Copyright © Callum MacDonald 1990

First published 1990

Basil Blackwell Ltd
108 Cowley Road, Oxford, OX4 1JF, UK

Basil Blackwell, Inc.
3 Cambridge Center
Cambridge, Massachusetts 02142, USA

All rights reserved. Except for the quotation of short passages for the
purposes of criticism and review, no part of this publication may be
reproduced, stored in a retrieval system, or transmitted, in any form or by any
means, electronic, mechanical, photocopying, recording or otherwise, without
the prior permission of the publisher.

Except in the United States of America, this book is sold subject to the
condition that it shall not, by way of trade or otherwise, be lent, re-sold,
hired out, or otherwise circulated without the publisher's prior consent in any
form of binding or cover other than that in which it is published and without
a similar condition including this condition being imposed on the subsequent
purchaser.

British Library Cataloguing in Publication Data

A CIP catalogue record for this book is available from the British Library.

Library of Congress Cataloging in Publication Data

MacDonald, C. A.
   Britain and the Korean War/Callum MacDonald.
      p. cm. — (Making contemporary Britain)
   Includes bibliographical references.
   ISBN 0−631−16769−2 — ISBN 0−631−16771−4 (pbk.):
   1. Korean War, 1950−1953 — Great Britain   I. Title.   II. Series.
DS919.3.M33   1990
951.904′2 — dc20   89−18128
                                                            CIP

Typeset in 11 on 13 pt Ehrhardt
by Setrite Typesetters
Printed in Great Britain by Billing & Sons Ltd, Worcester

Contents

General Editor's Preface

The Institute of Contemporary British History's series *Making Contemporary Britain* is aimed directly at students in schools and universities and at others interested in learning more about topics in post-war British history. In the series, authors are less attempting to break new ground than presenting clear and balanced overviews of the state of knowledge on each of the topics.

The ICBH was founded in October 1986 with the objective of promoting the study of British history since 1945 at every level. To that end, it publishes books and a quarterly journal, *Contemporary Record*; it organizes seminars and conferences for school students, undergraduates, researchers and teachers of post-war history; and it runs a number of research programmes and other activities.

A central theme of the ICBH's work is that post-war history is too often neglected in British schools, institutes of higher education and beyond. The ICBH acknowledges the validity of the arguments against the study of recent history, notably the problems of bias, of overly subjective teaching and writing, and the difficulties of perspective. But it believes that the values of studying post-war history outweigh the drawbacks, and that the health and future of a liberal democracy require that its citizens know more about the most recent past of their country than the limited knowledge possessed by British citizens, young and old, today. Indeed, the ICBH believes that the dangers of political indoctrination are higher where the young are *not* informed of the recent past.

Callum MacDonald's short book on the Korean War is timely because, despite a flurry of television programmes and books in the late 1980s, the war remains largely ignored in Britain. Its geographic remoteness, the war's comparative brevity and the fact of its being overshadowed by the recently ended Second World War all militate against its proper consideration. The book, it is hoped, will make the details of the causes, course and consequences of the war far more widely accessible. It is indeed, to date, the best brief account of Britain's involvement in the war.

Anthony Seldon

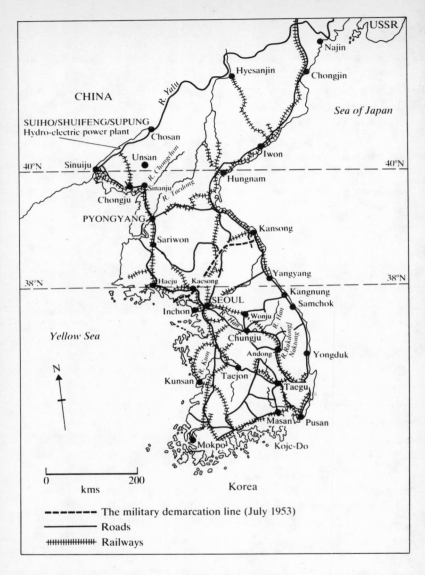

CHINA

USSR

SUIHO/SHUIFENG/SUPUNG
Hydro-electric power plant

Najin

Hyesanjin

Chongjin

Sea of Japan

Chosan

Unsan

R. Yalu

R. Chongchon

40°N

Sinuiju

Iwon

40°N

Sinanju

R. Taedong

Hungnam

Chongju

PYONGYANG

Kansong

Sariwon

38°N

Haeju

Kaesong

Yangyang

38°N

SEOUL

Kangnung

Inchon

Wonju

Samchok

Yellow Sea

R. Han

R. Han

Chungju

R. Rakdong/
Naktong

N

Andong

Yongduk

Kunsan

R. Kum

Taejon

Taegu

Masan

Pusan

Mokpol

Koje-Do

Korea

0   200
    kms

- - - - - - - The military demarcation line (July 1953)
───────── Roads
╫╫╫╫╫╫╫ Railways

The map of Korea is reproduced from *Korea: The War Before Vietnam*
by Callum MacDonald (1986), by kind permission of The Macmillan
Press, London.

1 The Reason Why

The special relationship and the cold war

In the basement of the Victorious Fatherland Liberation War Museum in Pyongyang, the capital of North Korea, a solitary British Bren gun carrier stands amongst the ranks of captured American equipment, a mute reminder of British participation in a distant Asian war fought under the banner of the United Nations. Britain had no direct strategic or economic interest in Korea and before 1950 the British public hardly knew of its existence. Winston Churchill later complained that he had 'never heard of the bloody place' until he was seventy-four.[1] Yet within days of the outbreak of war the government had committed naval forces to the fighting, followed shortly afterwards by two infantry brigades and supporting arms, which ultimately served as part of a British Commonwealth Division. This military contribution, although modest compared with those of the United States and the Republic of Korea, strained British resources and was the second largest amongst the sixteen members of the United Nations which participated in the war.

Britain's involvement in the Korean conflict sprang directly from the cold war and the central role of the 'special relationship' with the United States in British foreign policy. In London, as in Washington, the North Korean attack was regarded as a Soviet initiative. Since 1945 the Labour government of Clement Attlee had feared Soviet expansion and defined a close alliance with the United States as vital to British security and the maintenance of Britain's position as a great power. It followed the example of Churchill's wartime coalition, which had adopted a policy of becoming 'mixed up together' with the Americans as the key to national survival in the conflict with Nazi Germany. Churchill distrusted Soviet intentions even during the wartime Grand Alliance with Russia, and well before the Potsdam conference in 1945 was pressing the United States to stand up to Stalin in negotiations amongst the Big Three. Churchill hoped to call in the new world to redress the balance of the old, fearing a post-war American retreat into isolationism, which would leave an exhausted Britain to face the Soviet Union alone across the ruins of Hitler's Reich. He made little progress, however, with President Franklin D. Roosevelt, who was committed to a vision of a post-war international order based on cooperation with Russia.

Despite Churchill's election defeat in 1945 there was a strong element of continuity in British foreign policy. As recent studies have emphasized, on the Western side it was Britain and not the United States that moved first towards cold war with the Soviet Union. Churchill's approach was rapidly adopted by Attlee's Labour government and its Foreign Secretary, Ernest Bevin. Bevin suspected Soviet designs but soon realized that Britain lacked the strength to hold the ring on its own. His aim was to mobilize American resources behind British interests and guarantee the survival of Britain as a great power by committing the United States to the containment of communism. By the end of 1946 this approach was paying off as relations between Washington and Moscow deteriorated under Roosevelt's successor, Harry S. Truman. Bevin played a leading role in each step towards the construction of the US containment system, from the Marshall Plan of 1947 to the NATO alliance of 1949.

As the cold war intensified, Bevin was able to exploit the personal and institutional contacts established during the Second World War to consolidate the Anglo-American alliance. Although Attlee and Truman never enjoyed the informal relationship achieved between Churchill and Roosevelt, the United States worked more closely with Britain than with any other country. Bevin distrusted Truman's first Secretary of State,

James F. Byrnes, whom he considered too soft with the Russians, but established good relations with his successors, George Marshall and Dean Acheson. At a lower level the British ambassador to the United States, Oliver Franks, appointed in 1948, was an influential figure. When Acheson first became Secretary of State, he invited Franks to talk with him confidentially at any time about international problems. Military contacts also existed in the shape of the British Joint Services Mission in Washington, headed by Air Marshal Lord Tedder, which provided liaison between the British Chiefs of Staff and the Pentagon.

Bevin's aim was to overcome the legacy of isolationism and establish the 'special relationship' as the basic element in US global strategy, an approach that enjoyed broad bipartisan support. Like many of his officials he regarded the United States as a well-intentioned but inexperienced colossus in need of guidance by those better versed in world politics. The Atlantic alliance would combine British experience with American power. The attitude was well expressed by a piece of anonymous doggerel written during the Anglo-American loan negotiations of 1945 when British dependence on US economic assistance was clearly revealed:

> In Washington Lord Halifax
> Once whispered to Lord Keynes:
> It's true *they* have the money bags
> But *we* have all the brains.[2]

So anxious was Bevin to lay the ghost of isolationism that during the Berlin crisis in 1948, he allowed the United States to base strategic bombers in East Anglia without any formal agreement guaranteeing Britain's right to consultation before the airfields were employed operationally. According to the US officer in charge of the bomber squadrons, such an arrangement was unprecedented. Bevin regarded the NATO alliance of 1949 as one of his most important achievements, since it committed the United States to the defence of Western Europe for the first time.

As American observers noted, Bevin's approach assumed the

identity of British and US interests in an attempt to compensate for Britain's declining power in the world. If the British regarded the 'special relationship' as a prop for their threatened position, however, what the Americans wanted out of it was 'support for their hegemony'.[3] Britain was rigorously excluded from one area vital to that hegemony, the atomic bomb, despite Anglo-American cooperation in its development during the war. After 1945 Britain lost its veto over the employment of the 'winning weapon' and was denied access to American atomic research as Washington attempted to create a US monopoly. In order to maintain great-power status Britain embarked on its own atomic programme, but a British bomb was not successfully tested until October 1952. British influence over American employment of atomic weapons was to become an important issue during the Korean War, when the world seemed to hover on the brink of global conflict. In this atmosphere the related issue of control over US bases was also to assume a new urgency as the Americans deployed B-29 bombers, equipped with atomic weapons, to Britain in readiness for possible war with Russia.

By 1950, therefore, the Labour government had moved inescapably into the economic, political and military orbit of the United States. As the American ambassador to London, Lewis Douglas, emphasized in 1948, although Anglo-American unity was more firmly established than ever before in peacetime, the 'special relationship' was not a partnership of equals. The fate of Britain rested largely on decisions taken in Washington, and almost every day brought new evidence of this dependence. When Truman drew the line against communist aggression in Korea the British reaction was thus inevitable. As Attlee concluded: 'We'll have to support the Yanks'.[4]

The shadow of Munich

This imperative was reinforced by the lessons of the past. Korea had a symbolic significance as the first case of armed expansion since 1945. The experience of the 1930s shaped the responses of British policy-makers and provided their terms of reference. The history of that unhappy decade appeared to demonstrate the dangers of appeasing aggression by totalitarian regimes. According to this argument, the concessions made to Hitler at Munich in 1938 had merely whetted the dictator's appetite for more and led directly to the Second World War. If another such conflict was to be avoided, it was vital to take a strong stand from the beginning. If communist aggression in Korea went unpunished, Stalin might be encouraged to try again in areas of greater strategic significance. In this situation it seemed vital to support collective security through the United Nations. At that stage, when the UN was dominated by the United States and its allies, leaders like Attlee and Truman found no difficulty in regarding it as an important tool in the cold war, lending moral authority to the policy of containment. According to the Prime Minister, the new world organization must not be allowed to go the way of the old League of Nations, an argument which had a strong appeal only five years after the defeat of Hitler.

Conclusions

Britain went to war in 1950 to consolidate the Anglo-American alliance and to resist communist aggression, goals which were inextricably linked in the minds of the men who made policy. Their decision owed nothing to the direct importance of Korea itself to British interests. For the next three years Britain was to fight *in* but not *for* Korea, often displaying scant regard for Korean wishes and interests as it pursued these larger goals.

Notes

1 Callum A. MacDonald, *Korea: The War Before Vietnam* (London 1986), p. 187.
2 Robin Edmonds, *Setting The Mould: The United States and Britain 1945–1950* (London 1986), p. 100.

3 Ra Jong-yil, 'Special Relationship at War: The Anglo-American Relationship during the Korean War', in *The Journal of Strategic Studies*, vol. 7, no. 3, September 1984, p. 315.
4 Kenneth Harris, *Attlee* (London 1982), p. 454.

2 Background to the Conflict

Korea and the cold war

The Korean War began on 25 June 1950 when the North Korean People's Army crossed the 38th parallel in an attempt to crush South Korea and unify the peninsula under the communist regime of Kim Il Sung (see map, p. viii). This attack, regarded by the West as an example of Soviet imperialism, was rooted in events which followed the liberation of Korea from Japan in 1945. When Japan surrendered, the United States proposed, and the Soviet Union accepted, the 38th parallel as the demarcation line between occupation zones in Korea. Although the parallel was soon to divide two hostile Korean states, each linked to opposing ideological blocs, the arrangement was originally regarded as a temporary expedient. At the Moscow Foreign Ministers' Conference in December 1945 the United States and the Soviet Union agreed on the creation of a Korean provisional government followed by a short period of international trusteeship by America, Russia, Britain and China leading to independence. As a first step a joint commission of the local US and Soviet military commands was to consult with Korean democratic parties and social groups.

The Moscow Agreement, however, was never implemented. It represented the last gasp of a policy of international cooperation first proposed by President Franklin D. Roosevelt at the Cairo Conference of 1943 and discussed with the Russians at Tehran and Yalta. Roosevelt's plans for Korea reflected his wider aim of incorporating the Soviet Union into an American-dominated world order by giving the Russians a stake in the system, a policy known as containment by inclusion. As this vision disintegrated in the post-war period under his successor, Harry S. Truman, Korea became a victim of the cold war. It was a development for which the Korean people, scarcely liberated from generations of Japanese occupation, were to pay a terrible price.

When the Moscow Agreement was signed, separate administrations were already emerging on either side of the 38th parallel. The US and Soviet forces that entered Korea found a country in the throes of revolution. This was dominated by the left, popular because of its long record of opposition to Japanese rule. In the north the Russians supported the communists and backed the faction led by Kim Il Sung, a young man who had first made his name as an anti-Japanese guerrilla during the 1930s. In the south the US military government, under General Hodge, identified the Korean revolution with Soviet imperialism. The American command embraced the right and promoted Syngman Rhee, an aging nationalist brought back from exile in the United States to provide popular leadership for a group tainted by collaboration with Japanese colonialism. The result was civil war as the police and paramilitary groups were unleashed against the left in the American zone. This development undermined any hope of creating a provisional government, since it proved impossible for the US–Soviet joint commission to agree on which Korean groups to consult. Although Washington attempted to disown Hodge's early alliance with the right and build a moderate coalition behind the Moscow Agreement in 1946, this effort was doomed by the polarization of Korean politics. The actions taken in the first months of the occupation had 'compromised ... later efforts at conciliation and cooperation between Left and Right, or between the United States and the Soviet Union'.[1]

The final collapse of the wartime alliance between America and Russia was signalled by the proclamation of the Truman Doctrine in March 1947 and the launching of the Marshall Plan for the economic recovery of Western Europe three months later. These events accelerated the division of Europe into hostile blocs and had repercussions in distant Korea where a second round of joint commission talks ended in deadlock. The formal opening of the cold war forced Washington to consider its global priorities. Big budgets were unpopular and there were limits to what Congress would spend in the cause of containment. In this situation it was decided to concentrate available resources on Europe, the most vital theatre in the confrontation with communism. In the Far East the United States would hold a line of offshore strongpoints, stretching from the Japanese home islands, through Okinawa to the Philippines, and minimize commitments on the Asian mainland. Direct military involvement in the Chinese civil war between the Guomindang (Kuomintang) regime of Generalissimo Jiang Jieshi (Chiang Kai-shek) and the communists under Mao, which had broken out in 1946, would be avoided. Jiang's regime had proved too weak and corrupt, despite a decade of US aid, to be considered a viable instrument of containment. Instead the Americans would rebuild their former enemy Japan as the central pillar of the Asian security system. The expensive US military government in Korea would be liquidated. According to the Joint Chiefs of Staff (JCS), Korea was strategically unimportant in the event of global war, and American troops could be better employed elsewhere. The low strategic value of Korea, however, conflicted with its high symbolic importance. Korea was the only place in Asia where the United States directly confronted the Soviet Union, and a withdrawal which produced a victory for the left would endanger American credibility. Rather than risk a communist Korea, Washington was prepared to accept half a loaf: the permanent division of the peninsula.

The United Nations and partition

In September 1947 Washington took the Korean problem to the General Assembly of the United Nations and proposed elections for a national convention representing north and south, followed by the creation of a government and the withdrawal of foreign troops. The Soviet bloc opposed the plan, but the

United States and its allies dominated the General Assembly, where the veto enjoyed by the Russians on the Security Council did not apply. On 14 November 1947 a United Nations Temporary Commission on Korea (UNTCOK) was established despite Soviet objections, a step which made partition inevitable. UNTCOK was refused entry into the north and discovered that all shades of political opinion in the south, except for the far right, opposed a separate election below the 38th parallel. There were also doubts about the legitimacy of such elections, given Rhee's control of the police and the prevailing atmosphere of political repression. In these circumstances the commission referred the problem back to the General Assembly where, after American lobbying, it was decided that UNTCOK should observe elections in such parts of Korea as were accessible. The poll which followed in May 1948 was pronounced valid by UNTCOK despite the continuing reservations of some delegates. A government was organized under Rhee, and on 12 December 1948 the UN General Assembly recognized the new Republic of Korea (ROK) with its capital in Seoul. Meanwhile, in September 1948 the Democratic People's Republic of Korea (DPRK) was established in Pyongyang under Kim Il Sung and recognized by the Soviet bloc. By December the last Russian troops had been withdrawn, leaving behind a group of advisors with the North Korean People's Army (NKPA). The failure of the Moscow Agreement had thus institutionalized a civil war in two hostile states north and south of the 38th parallel each claiming to represent all Koreans.

Despite US economic and military support, the ROK was an unstable creation. It was shaken by guerrilla uprisings and an army mutiny at Yosu, which was only put down after heavy fighting. There were also armed clashes with the NKPA along the 38th parallel. The situation was bad enough to delay the withdrawal of the last US troops until the summer of 1949. For Washington, Rhee proved a difficult ally and there was constant friction over his failure to control inflation and his dictatorial political methods. He also caused concern by making no secret of his desire to reunite Korea by force of arms. The Americans did not wish to be dragged into a war by Rhee and denied him the type of armaments required to march north. The ROK Army shaped by US military advisors was chiefly an anti-guerrilla force and lacked tanks or heavy artillery. The Americans hoped to deter a direct attack on the south by a policy of deliberate ambiguity which invoked the United Nations. A new UN Commission on Korea (UNCOK) was created in December 1948, which later sent military observers to monitor the situation along the 38th parallel. In January 1950 the US Secretary of State, Dean Acheson, made a speech defining a strategic perimeter in Asia based on island strongpoints. The mainland states would receive American military and economic aid but must look to the UN as their first defence. This was not an expression of uninterest in the fate of the ROK, but part of a continuing policy of containment 'on the cheap' beyond the island line.

Britain and the United States in the Far East

Britain emerged from the Second World War with commitments which outstripped resources. British strategic priorities in the early cold war lay in Europe and the Middle East. In Asia, the south-east was regarded as the most vital region. While Anglo-American relations were close in Europe, there was less co-operation in the Far East where British officials were critical of US policy. According to the Foreign Secretary, Ernest Bevin, the Americans had been 'a law unto themselves' in the area since 1945, often with unhappy results.[2] From the British perspective, US policy in Asia seemed peculiarly vulnerable to the influence of domestic politics and bureaucratic rivalries, factors which made it volatile and unpredictable. The government was particularly critical of the American position on China which seemed almost wholly dictated by the public emotions whipped up by the right wing of the Republican party in the wake of the communist victory in the civil war in October 1949.

In January 1950 Britain recognized the new People's Republic of China established by Mao. Bevin wished to preserve British economic interests and to safeguard the position of Hong Kong, which was vulnerable to Chinese pressure. Other considerations were also involved. Bevin feared the impact of the communist victory on Asia and in particular on the situation in Indochina. While the Western position had to be strengthened to prevent the spread of revolution in the area, however, Bevin believed that the new China was more nationalist than communist and might eventually break with Russia if allowed an opening to the West. Isolation would merely drive Beijing closer to Moscow and prevent the development of more moderate policies. This approach was based partly on the example of Yugoslavia, which had broken with the Soviet Union in 1947, and partly on the British experience in India, which had been granted its independence after the war. The British believed that their long connection with India granted them a unique insight into Asian nationalism and qualified them to lecture the Americans on the subject, an approach that was resented in Washington. India was and remained a strong influence on British policy towards China. Bevin wished to placate India, which he regarded as the leader of Asian opinion, and to maintain the unity of the Commonwealth. The Indian leader, Jawaharlal Nehru, made it clear that he would oppose any attempt to isolate China, and regarded India as a bridge between the communist regime and the West. Washington, however, continued to recognize Jiang's discredited Guomindang regime, which had fled to the island of Taiwan (Formosa), and showed little concern for Indian sensibilities. The Foreign Office attributed Washington's reluctance to jettison Jiang to domestic political pressures stirred up by right-wing Republicans anxious to discredit the Democratic administration in the wake of Truman's unexpected victory in the 1948 presidential elections. For their part, many Americans regarded British policy as the product of an unholy alliance between the economic self-interest of the City and the ideology of the Labour left. These differences over China were to grow into a major source of friction with the outbreak of the Korean War.

By contrast with China, a measure of Anglo-American agreement had begun to emerge on south-east Asia by the end of

1949. Britain argued that American support was essential to prevent the spread of communism there, in the wake of the Chinese revolution, most notably in Indochina where the French were engaged in a colonial war against the Vietminh under Ho Chi Minh. It was believed in London that the fall of Indochina would produce a domino effect throughout the region and complicate Britain's problems in Malaya, where a communist insurgency had broken out in 1948. At the beginning of 1950 Washington began a programme of economic and military aid to Indochina, a move which was welcomed by London, and both powers recognized the French-sponsored regime of Bao Dai as a nationalist alternative to the communists. Thereafter the Americans seemed prepared to consult the British about further moves to promote economic development in south-east Asia and to encourage cooperation amongst the nations of the region, a trend which Bevin found encouraging.

In north-east Asia the situation was very different. The main British priority in the area was promoting an international peace treaty with Japan, but the occupation was controlled by the Americans, who were slow to act, primarily because of bureaucratic rivalries in Washington. Korea was regarded as unimportant, and British officials showed little understanding of, or sympathy for, Korean nationalism. Although Bevin signed the Moscow Agreement in 1945, he was anxious to avoid direct involvement in the volatile politics of the peninsula. The Foreign Office was sceptical about the prospects of trusteeship and the capacity of Koreans for self-government. While British officials sometimes complained about lack of consultation by the Americans, Britain was content to let Washington make the running in an area where geography gave the Russians a natural advantage. As a result Britain had little influence on the events which led to partition. When the Americans decided to withdraw their forces, they acted on their own. It was assumed in London that the resort to the United Nations was 'a face-saving formula' designed to allow Washington to reduce its commitment without loss of dignity.[3] The Foreign Office doubted the ability of the ROK to survive and felt scant sympathy for the 'unpopular and ... not very democratic' regime of Syngman Rhee.[4] An open North Korean attack across the 38th parallel was not expected, but rather the eventual collapse of the ROK from within as a result of Rhee's mismanagement and communist subversion. It was assumed that in such an event the Americans would stand aside, since Korea was of no strategic value in the event of a third world war.

The eve of war

US policy, however, was beginning to change. As the Republican political attack gathered strength after the fall of China, it was clear that the Truman administration could not afford to let another Asian country fall to communism. This would give ammunition to the Republican opposition and might endanger the whole programme of aid to Europe, the main priority in the cold war. In February 1950 Senator Joseph McCarthy launched his first charges of communism in the State Department which were to become a major theme in the Republican campaign. Moreover, there was increasing concern about the international credibility of the United States following the first successful test of a Soviet atomic bomb in September 1949 and the triumph of the Chinese communists one month later. It was feared in Washington that the United States was losing the initiative in the cold war and that with the atomic monopoly broken, American determination to resist communism was in doubt. As a result a new containment policy began to emerge in early 1950 which was embodied in a document known as NSC-68.

NSC-68 defined the Soviet Union as an inherently expansive totalitarian state, like Nazi Germany, which aimed at world conquest. It abandoned the distinction between vital and peripheral areas in the cold war and called on the United States to resist communism everywhere. It assumed that possession of the atomic bomb would make the Kremlin bolder and increase the danger of world war. By 1954 Russia would be in a position to wage global war against the United States, perhaps initiating hostilities by a surprise attack. Alternatively, Stalin might utilize the emerging atomic stalemate to employ his superior conventional forces or those of his satellites around the periphery of the Soviet bloc. NSC-68 called for massive rearmament by the United States and its allies to meet this threat, arguing that the only way to deal with Moscow was from a position of overwhelming military strength. The survey was submitted to Truman in April 1950 but was not approved by the President. The administration was waiting for a crisis to sell the costly new programmes involved to an economy-minded congress.

In the wake of NSC-68 there were signs that the United States intended to draw firmer lines against communism in the Far East. The change was clearest on the issue of Taiwan. In January 1950 Truman had announced that the United States would not intervene to prevent the fall of the island to the Chinese communists and save the Guomindang. The administration did not like the new regime in Beijing but recognized the political bankruptcy of Jiang. Acheson hoped that China would eventually prove more nationalist than communist, creating strains in the Sino-Soviet relationship that could be exploited by the United States. Although the Americans opposed British recognition of the Beijing regime in January 1950, differences in the China policies of the two countries were then more apparent than real. Washington wanted to delay its own move both for domestic political reasons and because it was unwilling to run after communists. The American position, however, soon began to change. While domestic politics played a part, the administration also seemed to have become convinced that the new China was simply a Russian satellite, a view encouraged by the signature of the Sino-Soviet pact in February 1950 and the recognition by both communist powers of Ho Chi Minh's Democratic Republic of Vietnam. By the early summer Washington was considering some means of permanently denying Taiwan to the Chinese communists, reflecting the thinking which lay behind NSC-68. The Foreign Office recognized the seeds of trouble in this development. It not only abrogated the Cairo Declaration of 1943, which defined Taiwan as an integral part of China, but also threatened the prospects of a common Anglo-American policy towards Beijing. These fears were to be confirmed with the outbreak of the Korean War.

The existence of NSC-68 made a strong US reaction inevitable when the North Koreans attacked on 25 June 1950, despite earlier American reservations about defending South Korea. Although a build-up of the NKPA along the 38th parallel was detected in the spring, the Americans regarded tension there as routine and assumed that Russian priorities lay in other areas. In fact the decision to attack the ROK owed more to Korean politics than to any plan drawn up by the Kremlin. It is clear that the initiative came from Kim Il Sung rather than Stalin, whose role was restricted to supplying, at a price, the tanks and aircraft required by the NKPA. It was assumed by the North Koreans either that the United States would not intervene or that they could score a quick victory before Washington was able to react. This proved to be a fundamental miscalculation. The North Korean attack was regarded as a Soviet challenge by an administration already sensitive about its credibility at home and abroad. Truman's reaction was to involve the United States and its allies in a bitter struggle for a country whose significance was more symbolic than real, with unforeseen consequences for both Washington and London.

Conclusions

After the Second World War the Anglo-American 'special relationship' was more evident in Europe than in the Far East, where the United States tended to act unilaterally, a reflection of the decline of British power in the area since 1939. Britain was often frustrated by its inability to influence American decisions and critical of US policy, particularly over China which began to emerge as a source of friction after British recognition of the communist regime in January 1950. As for Korea, Britain played no direct part in the developments which set the stage for war, and the subject was never discussed by the cabinet in the eighteen months before June 1950. The conflict in this obscure corner of north-east Asia, however, was to have important consequences for the Anglo-American alliance and for the future of the Labour government.

Notes

1 Bruce Cumings, 'American Policy and Korean Liberation', in Frank Baldwin (ed.), *Without Parallel: The American—Korean Relationship Since 1945* (New York 1974), p. 85.
2 Ritchie Ovendale, 'Britain and the Cold War in Asia', in Ritchie Ovendale (ed.), *The Foreign Policy of the British Labour Governments 1945—1951* (Leicester 1984). p. 133.
3 Peter Lowe, *The Origins of the Korean War* (London 1986), p. 46.
4 H.M.G.J. Gladwyn, *The Memoirs of Lord Gladwyn* (London 1972), p. 228.

3 The Korean Decisions

Washington intervenes

When the NKPA crossed the 38th parallel the Americans
were taken by surprise. Their reaction, however, was swift.
The North Korean attack was regarded as a Soviet probe
with global implications. A firm line had to be drawn against
totalitarian aggression if the world was not to relive the
dismal experiences of the thirties. On 25 June the United
States took the issue to the United Nations and in the
absence of the Russians, who were boycotting the Security
Council over its refusal to seat the communists as the representatives of China, secured a resolution condemning North
Korea and demanding the withdrawal of the NKPA behind
the 38th parallel. On 27 June the Security Council passed a
second American resolution calling on all members of the
UN to aid the ROK in repelling aggression. The same day
Truman announced the commitment of US air and naval
forces in support of the South Koreans. According to the
President the attack made it 'plain beyond all doubt that
Communism has passed beyond the use of subversion to
conquer independent nations and will now use armed invasion
and war'.[1]

When air and naval support proved insufficient, Truman
took the final step and despatched ground forces from the US
Eighth Army in Japan. By a third Security Council resolution
on 7 July a UN Command (UNC) was established under
the American commander in the Far East, General Douglas

MacArthur, which included all UN contingents fighting in Korea and also the ROK forces. Truman argued that the world organization as well as the United States had been challenged by the communists. Its prestige must be upheld. The UN flag, however, hid the reality of American power. In the absence of the Soviet Union, the United States was able to employ the Security Council as an instrument in the cold war. As for the UNC, MacArthur took his orders, not from the UN, but from Truman and the JCS in Washington.

In the wake of the attack, the Americans drew the line against communism not only in Korea but also throughout the Far East. US action outside Korea was taken unilaterally and did not involve the UN. On 27 June Truman announced increased aid to the Philippines and Indochina and the 'neutralization' of Taiwan by the US 7th Fleet. Truman justified the Taiwan decision on security grounds, citing the need to protect the flanks of US forces operating in Korea. According to the President the future status of the island 'must await the restoration of security in the Pacific, a peace settlement with Japan or consideration by the United Nations'.[2] In fact the move reflected growing concern in Washington about communist China, and a desire to deny the island permanently to Mao and his Soviet allies. Some kind of American initiative had been under consideration since the late spring in the wake of NSC-68. Truman's decision was also influenced by domestic politics and Republican demands for firm action to save Taiwan. Although described as 'neutralization' which prevented Jiang from attacking the mainland as well as the communists from seizing Taiwan, Truman's intervention favoured one side in the Chinese civil war, since without the Americans the Guomindang faced extinction.

The British reaction

Britain, like the United States, was taken by surprise by the outbreak of war. On the eve of the North Korean attack the British minister in Seoul, Vyvyan Holt, reported that trouble was unlikely in the near future. Holt was shortly to become a prisoner of the advancing NKPA and would spend the next three years in captivity. There was little doubt in London that the Kremlin had connived at, if it had not instigated, the North Korean action. Britain had no direct strategic interest in Korea, but recognized that if the Russians succeeded there they might repeat the experiment in more vital areas such as Iran. The initiative, however, lay with the United States, and it was at first unclear whether Washington would do more than condemn the DPRK. When Truman drew the line on 27 June and committed US forces to the defence of the ROK, the cabinet supported the American position without a dissenting voice. The following day British naval units in the Far East were sent into battle as a symbol of British solidarity with the United States and the United Nations.

Attlee, like Truman, was influenced by the lessons of the thirties. As he explained in a broadcast on 23 July:

> The attack by the armed forces of North Korea on South Korea has been denounced as an act of aggression by the United Nations ... If the aggressor gets away with it, aggressors all over the world will be encouraged. The same results which led to the second world war will follow, and another world war may result. This is why what is happening in Korea is of such importance to you. The fire that has been started in distant Korea may burn down your own house.[3]

The emphasis on upholding the authority of the UN, however, was combined with a desire to maintain the alliance with the United States on which British security depended. It was considered important to give a lead to other members of the world organization and confirm Britain's position as America's most important ally. After the cabinet meeting on 27 June the Minister of Town and Country Planning, Hugh Dalton, noted the consensus that the Americans were calling the Russian bluff and that Britain must keep in line with them.

While the government supported UN intervention in Korea, it did not want to become involved in an open-ended military commitment in a peripheral area far from the centres of strategic importance in Europe and the Middle East. As Attlee argued on 6 July, the situation in Korea should not blind the West to the dangers nearer home. The Prime Minister proposed wide-ranging talks with the Americans to 'reach some agreement as to our common policy in these areas in the event of further outbreaks'.[4] Discussions were held in Washington between 20 and 24 July in which there was broad agreement on the impor-tance of limiting hostilities in the Far East and countering possible Soviet moves elsewhere. At the same time it proved impossible to avoid further British commitments to Korea. During the Washington talks, the Americans asked Britain to provide ground forces for MacArthur's command. The govern-ment had hoped that this situation would not arise, for British military resources were already overstretched. The Truman administration, however, wished to emphasize the UN aspect of the war by involving as many national contingents as possible. For domestic political reasons it also wanted to show the American people that they were not bearing the burden of the fighting alone. According to the chairman of the JCS, General Omar Bradley, a gesture was more important than the early despatch of British troops. The ambassador in Washington, Oliver Franks, strongly advised the government to acquiesce, warning that a negative response would seriously impair the Anglo-American relationship. His advice was accepted on 24 July, when Britain announced that it was committing a brigade to the UN command. The decision stripped Britain's remaining military capacity and forced the recall of Second World War reservists, many of whom had just established themselves in peacetime occupations.

The formation and equipping of the 29th Brigade was a slow process. In the meantime, Britain faced fresh demands for a more immediate commitment, which were dictated by the in-creasingly desperate military situation in Korea. When the Truman administration sent in ground troops at the beginning of the war, it assumed that they would rapidly contain and drive back the advancing NKPA. This proved to be a fundamental misjudgement. American forces found themselves facing a tough and determined enemy who soon threatened to sweep them from Korea. The British Chiefs of Staff feared that the United States might be tempted to use the atomic bomb, and the possibility was indeed canvassed by MacArthur in mid-July. By the beginning of August over 90% of the country was in communist hands, and the US Eighth Army, along with surviving ROK forces, had retreated into a narrow perimeter behind the Rakdong (Naktong) River around the port of Pusan at the south-eastern tip of the peninsula (see map, p. viii).

In this situation the United States was compelled to strip its slim military reserves simply to avoid a humiliating defeat, and put pressure on its allies to step up their own commitment to the Korean fighting. According to MacArthur, his command was losing 500 men a day and lacked trained infantry. The immediate commitment of a British brigade might turn the tide and would be worth more than an entire division later. On 16 August General Bradley raised the question with the British military mission in Washington. The following day the government decided to accept the American demand for infantry and the 27th Brigade was hurriedly formed from the garrison of Hong Kong and despatched to Pusan. These British troop commitments were made reluctantly and justified on political rather than military grounds. By acting as a loyal ally Britain hoped to consolidate its influence in Washington. Failure to support the Truman administration in its hour of need might lead the American people to question the value of alliances and revert to isolationism with painful consequences for the defence of Europe. At that stage nobody could afford to take US assistance for granted.

Rearmament

The Korean War seemed to demonstrate the danger of armed communist expansion and offered the Truman administration the opportunity to launch NSC-68. The first increases in the US military budget were announced in July, and in September NSC-68 was formally adopted as a statement of national policy. Britain tried to keep in step with the Americans and give a lead to others. It was accepted in London that the dangers of aggression had increased and that Britain was in a poor position to fight Russia or resist communist probes in places like Germany or Iran. On 24 July the British Defence Secretary, Emmanuel Shinwell, proposed the first increases in the military budget, and at the beginning of August the cabinet committed itself to an additional defence expenditure of £3,400 million over three years. The period of national service was extended from eighteen months to two years. It was hoped that Washington would provide financial assistance for this programme, which was designed as the British contribution to a common Western defence effort in the new situation created by communist aggression in Korea. The war also raised the question of German rearmament and the relationship of West Germany to NATO. On 12 September the United States proposed the creation of an integrated NATO command which included German troops. If this was accepted the Truman administration was prepared to send additional US forces to Europe. Although the Attlee government had reservations about German rearmament, it was accepted in principle as the price of a greater American commitment to Europe and financial support for British rearmament. In the event real progress on German rearmament was blocked by the French and by the end of the year Washington had been forced to accept compromises.

The war and the home front

The government recognized that rearmament involved economic sacrifices. On 31 July Attlee warned the public that production would have to be diverted from consumption, but argued that it 'was well worth while to make some sacrifice of leisure now to prevent war'.[5] In the shock of the Korean emergency this message was accepted with little public debate. In the cabinet only Aneurin Bevan, the Minister of Health, expressed doubts about the militarization of the cold war and the shift in priorities from social and economic programmes to rearmament. The prevailing mood was captured by his colleague Hugh Dalton, who regretted the beginning of a new arms race but remarked that in the new situation created by Korea, Britain had no choice. Nor was there much debate about British participation in the Korean War and the despatch of troops, on which there was a bipartisan consensus. In the House of Commons the Conservative leader, Winston Churchill, pledged Attlee his full support. The lessons of the thirties and the dangers of appeasement were fresh in the public consciousness only five years after the defeat of Hitler. The involvement of the UN was particularly popular within the Labour Party, where only a small handful on the left rejected Attlee's endorsement of collective security. As Michael Foot argued in *Tribune*, the North Korean attack was 'an international crime of the first order' and the UN must be supported.[6] The party conference at Margate in October endorsed Attlee's decisions on Korea by a huge margin.

Support for the war survived potentially damaging reports about the nature of the ROK regime protected by the blue flag of the United Nations. As in all civil wars, the conflict in Korea was fought with a peculiar ferocity, and both sides were guilty of terrible atrocities. In the summer of 1950 the most visible were those committed by the Rhee regime. Before retreating the South Koreans often massacred political prisoners, while behind the lines the police waged an intense campaign against subversion. The situation sometimes shocked reporters and British troops fighting in Korea. The Foreign Office was sensitive to critical press comments and worked to keep them within bounds. The government argued that the real issue was not the nature of the Rhee regime, but resisting aggression, a line generally accepted by editors. The exception was the communist *Daily Worker*, which had a correspondent, Alan Winnington, with the advancing NKPA. In August 1950 Winnington reported the discovery of mass graves near Taejon containing the corpses of at least 7,000 men and women executed by ROK police. His article was published by his newspaper on 11 August under banner headlines and later appeared as a pamphlet entitled *I Saw The Truth In Korea*. The cabinet considered prosecuting Winnington and his editor for treason, since this and other articles critical of the war could be construed as giving aid and comfort to the enemy. In the end, however, it backed away from the legal and political problems involved.

The diplomacy of constraint – China and Taiwan

Although it supported the United States in Korea, the government was worried from the beginning that the Americans might go too far. Britain did not want to be dragged into a global war, nor did it want Washington to become so deeply embroiled in the Far East that the needs of Europe were neglected. As early as 27 July the cabinet expressed concern about Truman's draft speech announcing the commitment of American air and naval forces to Korea. The President planned to state that 'centrally directed communist imperialism' had resorted to armed attack, a phrase that ministers feared might back the Russians into a corner and make it difficult for Moscow to disown its satellite state without loss of face. If the Korean conflict were to be contained it was important to avoid throwing down a challenge that the Soviet Union might feel bound to take up.

Bevin was anxious to keep the Kremlin in play and, following a conversation between the British ambassador, Sir David Kelly, and the Soviet Deputy Foreign Minister, Andrei Gromyko, in early July toyed with the idea of promoting a general settlement in the Far East in return for a North Korean withdrawal behind the 38th parallel. This idea, however, was quickly quashed by Acheson, who made clear his opposition to any concessions to China involving Taiwan and the UN seat. During the Anglo-American talks held in Washington later in July, there was some dispute about Soviet readiness for war. While the British did not believe that the Russians would be fully prepared before 1955, the Americans favoured 1952 and argued that even before then Moscow would be ready to take serious risks. These, however, were minor disagreements. The Americans shared Britain's reluctance to contemplate global war, and Truman was careful to avoid pushing the Kremlin too far. The reinforcement of Strategic Air Command bases in

Britain by two wings of medium bombers was officially described as a training flight, and figures such as Francis Matthews, the US Secretary of the Navy, who embraced the notion of preventive war, were quickly dismissed.

The situation was different regarding China. Britain viewed with concern the American decision to 'neutralize' Taiwan, and the mission of the Royal Navy was strictly limited to resisting aggression in Korea. The Foreign Office refused to regard the Beijing regime as an obedient Soviet satellite. Bevin believed that at best Truman was driving the Chinese into the arms of the Russians and at worst risking a wider war in the Far East, which would divert resources from the more urgent requirements of Europe. He was particularly conscious of the danger of splitting the Commonwealth and the United Nations. While India supported collective security through the UN and sent a field ambulance to Korea, Nehru opposed US intervention in Taiwan, which he regarded as an act of old-fashioned imperialism. Bevin believed that the United States did not pay enough attention to Asian sensibilities. This was certainly true in the case of India. The Americans were contemptuous of Nehru's diplomacy, regarding him as an appeaser with a bad influence on British policy. Bevin also felt that the US position was unduly influenced by domestic politics and a desire to contain the right wing of the Republican party. As the Foreign Secretary remarked, he had his own political concerns. While the Labour Party was unanimous in supporting the UN action in Korea, many were less enthusiastic about US policy towards China. Although critical of Washington, Britain was careful to avoid any gesture which might alienate American public opinion. In deference to US pressure the government agreed in July to stricter controls on the export of strategic materials such as oil to China. As for Chinese membership of the UN, to which the United States remained hostile, Bevin informed Acheson that Britain would vote in favour of any UN resolution to seat communist China that was not connected with Korea. This was intended to reassure Washington that London would not support any Soviet move linking a Korean settlement with concessions to Beijing.

While Washington continued to emphasize Beijing's role as

an agent of the Soviet conspiracy in Asia, there was some evidence of American restraint in the summer of 1950. Barely holding on in Korea, the United States did not want to add to its troubles by further provoking China. General MacArthur visited Taiwan at the end of July, raising British concern about American intentions, and Washington announced a programme of military aid to the Guomindang, but the administration denied any intention of seeking a special position on the island or of encouraging Jiang to attack the mainland. When MacArthur issued a message to the Veterans of Foreign Wars in August that emphasized the strategic importance of Taiwan, he was forced to withdraw his statement by Truman. MacArthur had a reputation as a political general with his eye on the White House and the President believed that he was appealing to the Republicans at home. In the aftermath of this affair, Bevin suggested placing the Taiwan issue before the UN. The General Assembly would establish a committee that could decide when peace and security had returned to the Pacific, allowing the cession of the island to China. He recognized the difficulty of asking the administration to go any further when Taiwan was a divisive issue in domestic politics. Such a solution, however, might restrain China, please India and create a situation in which Britain could live with temporary 'neutralization'. Although Acheson was prepared to discuss this proposal, the two allies remained divided. In fact the administration had no intention of ever surrendering Taiwan but concealed this from the British.

Conclusions

In the initial stages of the Korean War the government moved quickly to support US action through the United Nations, a policy which enjoyed widespread popular support. This support extended to other measures introduced in the wake of the Korean crisis, such as the large rearmament programme announced in August 1950. The only political organization to challenge these moves was the British Communist Party and its paper the *Daily Worker*, which could be dismissed as tools of Soviet propaganda. The

Anglo-American 'special relationship' seemed to work well in the first months of the war. It was believed in Britain that loyal support for the United States in Korea would impress American public opinion with the value of alliances and thus ease the path of the Truman administration towards increased commitments in Europe, the vital theatre in the cold war. To stand on the sidelines would be to risk American disillusion with international commitments and a return to its isolationism of the thirties. While differences existed over China, they were not allowed to endanger the wider relationship. London believed that 'cooperation rather than confrontation would move Washington to moderate, if not modify, its policies'.[7] This was an assumption which was to be challenged when the war moved into its second phase.

Notes

1 Harry S. Truman, *Years of Trial and Hope* (New York 1956), p. 339.
2 Ibid.
3 Kenneth Harris, *Attlee* (London 1982), pp. 455−6.
4 Ibid., p. 454.
5 Ibid., p. 456.
6 Kenneth O. Morgan, *Labour in Power 1945−1951* (London 1985), p. 425.
7 Roger Dingman, 'Truman, Attlee and the Korean War Crisis', in Ian Nish (ed.), *The East Asian Crisis 1945−1951: The Problem of China, Korea and Japan*, International Studies Series 1982/1 (London 1982), p. 10.

4 Rollback — the March North

Crossing the 38th parallel

While MacArthur's forces were fighting with their backs to the sea at Pusan, officials in Washington were considering the objectives of US intervention. The issue was whether to restore the status quo shattered by the North Korean attack or to go further and reunite the peninsula by eliminating the DPRK. The dangers of the second course were obvious. Crossing the 38th parallel into the communist sphere of influence might provoke Soviet or Chinese intervention, leading to a wider war. The attractions, however, were also great if Soviet and Chinese intervention could be avoided. The elimination of the DPRK would roll back communism, punish aggression and increase the prestige of the United States throughout the Far East. It would pay dividends on the domestic front by refuting Republican charges that Truman was soft on communism in Asia, and ease the way towards the increased commitment to Europe that the administration was already contemplating. The debate over war aims was academic as long as the NKPA held the military initiative, but by the end of August, MacArthur had produced a plan to counter-attack by means of an amphibious landing far behind the North Korean lines at Inchon (see map, p. viii). This would recapture Seoul, cut enemy supply routes and catch the North Koreans between the landing force and Eighth Army breaking out of the Pusan perimeter. With its troops defeated in the South, the DPRK would be unable to resist an advance across the 38th parallel.

There were considerable doubts in Washington about the Inchon plan, which MacArthur himself admitted was a gamble. In the end, however, it was accepted by the JCS as the only alternative to the bloody stalemate along the Rakdong river. The prospect of victory in the south forced the administration to elaborate its thoughts on the future of Korea. These were encapsulated in NSC-81/1, approved by Truman on· 11 September four days before Inchon. NSC-81/1 envisaged military operations north of the 38th parallel to complete the defeat of the NKPA. Such operations, however, were contingent on Soviet and Chinese non-intervention. The United States would not fight a major war to reunify Korea. If an advance proved possible, the Soviet and Chinese frontiers were to be strictly respected. As a matter of policy, only ROK troops were to be used in the border provinces to avoid alarming Beijing and Moscow by deploying American forces in such sensitive areas.

As MacArthur had predicted, the Inchon landing was a stunning success. Despite the collapse of the NKPA and the recapture of Seoul, there was no sign that either Russia or China would intervene to save Kim Il Sung. The result was inevitable. On 27 September, swept forward by victory, the administration ordered MacArthur to cross the 38th parallel, basing his military directive on the provisions of NSC-81/1. Washington also moved to secure UN approval for its new policy of rollback, considering it important to maintain the moral backing of the world organization. The Americans had to act through the General Assembly, for the Soviet Union had resumed its seat on the Security Council in August and would undoubtedly have vetoed any move there. An appropriate resolution, drafted by Britain, was presented to the Political Committee on 30 September. It called for 'all appropriate steps to be taken to ensure conditions of stability throughout Korea' and for elections under UN supervision to create 'a unified, independent and democratic government'.[1] UN forces would remain in Korea only until these aims had been fulfilled, and a new UN Commission for the Unification and Rehabilitation of Korea (UNCURK) was to be established to supervise the process. The resolution did not explicitly sanction the use of force to attain UN goals. Nevertheless it gave tacit approval to the crossing of the parallel, since its provisions could only be enforced in the north at the point of a bayonet.

Britain and rollback

The British were also tempted by the vision of total victory and wished to keep in step with the Americans. The politicians, however, were more enthusiastic than the Chiefs of Staff, who remained ambivalent about military operations north of the 38th parallel. Bevin was in New York when the military situation was transformed by Inchon. On 21 September he was informed by Attlee that it was vital for the UN to establish itself as 'the deliverer not the destroyer of Korea'.[2] The world organization must assume responsibility for the rehabilitation of the whole country and forestall Russian intervention in the north. The Chinese would not be unhappy to see Soviet influence eliminated provided the UN nature of the exercise was emphasized. The Foreign Secretary replied the following day, agreeing on the need for swift action. According to Bevin the really tricky thing was to decide whether UN forces were to cross the 38th parallel, and a resolution had been drafted covering the issue. With no sign that the Kremlin intended to intervene, Bevin was determined to maintain the military and diplomatic initiative. As he emphasized on 25 September, if the UN accepted a return to the status quo 'Russia will have triumphed and the whole United Nations effort will have been in vain ... we must try to make sure now that just as in the case of the Berlin blockade the Russians are made to realise that they are up against it and to accept that fact'.[3] He hoped that the Indians could be persuaded to support UN action. In public Bevin stated that the artificial barrier of the 38th parallel must be swept away.

This attitude was at odds with the caution of the government earlier in the war, particularly in relation to China. Attlee and Bevin, however, believed that Korea, unlike Taiwan, was primarily a *Soviet* concern and that the Kremlin had decided to cut its losses there. China would not prolong the war and risk the hostility of the UN to rescue a defeated Russian satellite. Its best hope of international acceptance and the return of Taiwan lay in non-intervention. Beijing could be reassured about the security of its borders through the Indians and by careful wording of the UN resolution. In the last week in September, however, as MacArthur's forces approached the parallel, the Chinese began to issue warnings through · the Indian ambassador in Beijing, K.M. Panikkar, against any further advance. Although Nehru was alarmed, Britain was at first inclined to dismiss the statements as bluff. Only when the Chinese Foreign Minister, Zhou Enlai, summoned Panikkar from his bed on 2 October and bluntly stated that if US troops crossed the parallel, China would intervene, did London really react. Bevin, returning from New York on the *Queen Mary*, wired Acheson that Chinese intervention would be a great catastrophe and suggested offering Beijing a hearing at the General Assembly debate on Korea. The Chiefs of Staff, always ambivalent about the march north, were equally alarmed and emphasized the importance of limiting the war. There was no immediate military reason for crossing the parallel, and MacArthur's forces could halt for a short period while the Chinese position was explored. These sentiments were conveyed to the Defence Minister, Emmanuel Shinwell, and to Attlee, who was attending the party conference at Margate.

In the end, however, Attlee deferred to Bevin, and the Foreign Secretary advised caution. He believed that there was insufficient evidence to justify Indian fears that China would intervene. The Americans had already made it clear that they intended to go ahead in the face of what they regarded as a communist bluff. As a result representations in Washington would have to be at the highest level and in the strongest terms. If Britain did secure a pause in the fighting, it would be blamed for any subsequent military reverses. Bevin was clearly unwilling to damage Anglo-American relations and the prospect of increased US aid to Europe by adopting a position which might be regarded as appeasement. At the Labour Party conference he endorsed the decision to cross the parallel, arguing that UN intervention in Korea had created a precedent that would make aggressors think again. Privately, however, he emphasized the importance of limiting the war to Korea and avoiding any extension across the Yalu river into China. This reflected concern about the attitude of MacArthur, who informed a British diplomat in Tokyo on 3 October that he would bomb cities in Manchuria and north China, including Beijing, if China intervened. On 7 October the General Assembly passed the UN resolution on Korea and two days later the first American troops crossed the 38th parallel. Beijing denounced these moves as acts of aggression. Bevin, however, did not take such threats seriously and hoped that if China did cross the Yalu it would be with only token forces. Despite their belief that they understood Asian nationalism, the British as much as the Americans misjudged the Chinese reaction. Bevin argued that everything had been done to meet legitimate Chinese concerns by reassurances conveyed through India about the limited nature of UN military objectives, failing to understand the worthless- ness of such guarantees to China, which had endured a century of intervention and humiliation at the hands of foreigners. For the Chinese, there seemed little alternative but to fight to prevent the approach of American forces to the Manchurian border.

The march north

On 15 October Truman met MacArthur at Wake Island in the Pacific, an encounter that involved politics as much as strategy. As Franks noted, the President wished to associate himself publicly with the victor of Inchon in the run up to the November congressional elections. Before he left Washington, the British asked Truman to emphasize the vital importance of avoiding military reprisals outside Korea without the direct approval of the White House if Chinese forces intervened. They also ex- pressed the hope that they would be consulted in advance of such action. Franks implied that while Bevin trusted the Presi- dent, he had less confidence in the judgement of MacArthur, who had already created problems with China by his flamboyant gestures over Taiwan. At Wake, however, Truman was more concerned with the situation after the final defeat of the NKPA than with restrictions on MacArthur's operations. On the eve of his journey, Truman was informed by the Central Intelligence Agency (CIA) that the Chinese were unlikely to intervene, a judgement that was confirmed by MacArthur at their meeting. The general was convinced that the Korean campaign would be over by the end of November. He would begin redeploying US troops to Japan by Christmas and would have a division available for Europe early in the New Year. Truman returned to Washington convinced that the war was almost over. This seemed to be confirmed when the North Korean capital, Pyongyang, fell on 20 October. Four days later MacArthur ordered his troops to make full speed towards the Yalu. Although Washington queried this modification of his military directive, which called for the employment of only ROK troops in the frontier provinces, MacArthur was allowed to go ahead. With China apparently standing on the sidelines, precautions imposed at an earlier stage seemed unnecessary.

Rhee remained an embarrassment to the UN cause as victory approached. British reporters were often shocked by what they witnessed of the Korean civil war. Accounts began to appear in the British press of atrocities by ROK police both in the liberated south and beyond the 38th parallel. Don Greenlees of the *Daily Mirror* reported the savage beating of prisoners and routine executions of both men and women. According to the *Times* correspondent, Louis Heren, both sides acted with great brutality. The only difference was that the South Koreans were operating under the UN flag. At the beginning of November there was a Fleet Street scandal when the proprietor of *Picture Post* spiked an article by James Cameron, with photographs by Bert Hardy, on ROK atrocities. Cameron's piece, entitled 'An Appeal to the United Nations', condemned Rhee's tyranny and was implicitly critical of the Americans for supporting it. Questions about the situation were inevitably asked both by MPs and by members of organizations like the United Nations Association. While officials attempted to play down the incidence of atrocities, the government was concerned that the activities of the Rhee regime might undermine popular support for the war and alienate Asian countries, particularly India. Bevin was determined that the UN and not Rhee should exercise authority in the liberated north pending elections. On 28 October he raised the issue in Washington, briefly mentioning ROK atrocities. Bevin was reassured by the Americans on this point but received less satisfaction when he suggested supervised elections on both sides of the parallel to dispose of Rhee and create an entirely new government. Washington was unprepared to take any step that might cast doubt on the legitimacy of the ROK. This debate about the future of united Korea was soon to become academic.

China intervenes

Unknown to either Truman or MacArthur when they met at Wake, Chinese troops were already crossing the Yalu river. These forces, known as the Chinese People's Volunteers, were concentrated in the mountains in the path of the UN advance. By November 1950 there were 200,000 'volunteers' in Korea under General Peng Dehuai, a veteran of the Chinese civil war, reinforcing 80,000 NKPA remnants and guerrillas. Despite clashes with ROK troops at the end of October, their presence in force was not confirmed until the beginning of November when they attacked and destroyed an American regiment at Unsan, forcing Eighth Army to withdraw behind the Chongchon river (see map, p. viii). At the same time Chinese jet fighters, Mig-15s, appeared in the skies above north-west Korea. MacArthur's first instinct was to order the bombing of the international bridges across the Yalu to cut off the Chinese from their sources of supply. This move was countermanded by Washington, which insisted that only the North Korean ends of the bridges must be bombed to avoid attacking China. The Truman administration did not want to become involved in a wider war and began to look for ways of reassuring Beijing about the security of its borders. At the same time, however, it was sympathetic to MacArthur's demand for 'hot pursuit' of enemy aircraft into China to maintain air supremacy, a proposal which was only abandoned when it met with the universal hostility of the UN allies. The contradiction between this scheme and reassuring China went unnoticed in Washington, emphasizing the confusion which prevailed after the unexpected check to MacArthur's command.

Acheson favoured the creation of a narrow demilitarized zone on both sides of the Yalu to avoid a clash with China, a proposal discussed in Washington on 10 November. Although prepared to consider such a move, the administration was unwilling to suspend military operations. Chinese troops had vanished from the battlefield after Unsan, and both the scale and purpose of their intervention remained unclear. MacArthur's directive was to be kept under review, but the advance was to continue after UN forces had regrouped and built up their supplies. Britain was anxious to cooperate with the United States in restraining Beijing. On 10 November both powers supported a Security Council resolution confirming that UN policy was to 'hold the Chinese frontier with Korea inviolate and fully ... protect legitimate Chinese and Korean interests in the frontier zone'.[4] At the same time the Americans agreed that the Chinese should be invited to attend when the Security Council discussed MacArthur's report on Chinese intervention. The Chiefs of Staff, however, wanted Bevin to go further. They doubted whether MacArthur's forces could now reach the Yalu without bombing Manchuria and beginning a major war with China. According to a Russian source in Beijing, such a development would bring the Soviet airforce into the war. The Chiefs of Staff strongly urged a halt to military operations along the line Hungnam—Chongju, roughly around the 40th parallel, pending discussion of the problem at the UN. The area to the north of this line was to become a demilitarized zone (see map, p. viii).

The idea was put to Washington on 13 November. According to Bevin the demilitarized zone could be supervised by a UN commission in association with China, as a temporary measure pending Korean unification. In one sense it was a more rational proposal than the American idea of a narrower zone on either side of the Yalu but it failed to take the military situation into account. UN troops were well in advance of the proposed line on both sides of the peninsula and would have had to retreat. MacArthur had already made plain his opposition to any such arrangement, and the administration was not prepared to halt his advance. The Americans were convinced that political proposals should only be put forward from a position of strength. The United States must not appear to back down in the face of what might yet be a Chinese communist bluff. Although Acheson expressed interest in the British plan, he asked Bevin to postpone his initiative. The Foreign Secretary agreed. He had just rejected the American proposal for 'hot pursuit' on the advice of the Chiefs of Staff, who feared this would lead to the bombing of Manchuria, and did not want to risk a quarrel with Washington. Bevin realized that Truman was under great political pressure not to back down in the Far East following congressional elections in which right-wing Republicans had improved their position, and feared that an appearance of weakness in Asia might jeopardize the prospects of increased US aid to Europe.

In fact, the Americans had no intention of supporting the British plan and were moving away from their own limited scheme for a demilitarized zone on both sides of the Yalu. On 21 November it was decided in Washington to suggest that MacArthur halt his advance on the ridges overlooking the Yalu. The unoccupied strip would be lightly patrolled and entered in force by the UN command if Chinese troops were encountered there. When this mild restriction proved unacceptable to MacArthur, it was abandoned. The administration allowed itself to be carried forward both by MacArthur's continued belief in total victory and by its own opportunism. The continued absence of the Chinese from the battlefield encouraged the hope that a united Korea might yet be secured without either fighting the Chinese or negotiating with them. Despite his misgivings, Bevin deferred to the Americans. The idea of a demilitarized zone was later seen as a lost opportunity. Acheson's proposal for a zone on both sides of the Yalu, however, would have required the Chinese to abandon their own frontier. As for Bevin's alternative, it was unacceptable to Washington since it involved a retreat and risked giving Beijing something for nothing. There was in any case little sign of Chinese interest in such a compromise. The evidence suggests that by November 1950 it was too late for diplomatic solutions. Chinese troops had been withdrawn into the mountains after Unsan, not to allow time for negotiations, but to rest and regroup for the major battles to come.

Conclusions

As MacArthur later remarked, the decision to cross the 38th parallel was approved by everyone involved except the communists. The Attlee government, like the Truman administration, was tempted by the prospect of total victory, which might mark a turning point in the cold war. Although concerned by the Chinese warning delivered through Panikkar on 2 October, Bevin refused to break ranks when it became clear that Washington intended to go ahead regardless. In the last resort he was not prepared to risk the prospect of US support in Europe by opposing American policy in Korea. Such an approach would play into the hands of the Russians by splitting the Atlantic alliance. It would also provide ammunition for right-wing Republicans, no friends of Truman's NATO commitments, allowing them to characterize the British as appeasers unworthy of US support. Instead the government deferred to Washington and hoped for the best. For the same reasons, Bevin did not press the British plan for a demilitarized zone in November after the first clash with the Chinese People's Volunteers. In both cases the Chiefs of Staff were more concerned about the situation than the politicians, something later admitted by Bevin. By then, however, it was too late. The Chinese had entered the fighting in force, facing Washington and its allies with an entirely new war.

Notes

1 Denis Stairs, *The Diplomacy of Constraint: Canada, the Korean War and the United States* (Toronto 1975), p. 121.

2 Attlee to Bevin, 21 September 1950, FK1022/324 FO371/84097, Public Record Office, Kew, London.

3 Callum A. MacDonald, *Korea: The War Before Vietnam* (London 1986), p. 51.

4 Peter N. Farrar, 'A Pause for Peace Negotiations: The British Buffer Zone Plan of November 1950', in James Cotton and Ian Neary (eds), *The Korean War in History* (Manchester 1989), p. 68.

5 Crisis

Defeat in the North

On 24 November 1950 MacArthur launched his final offensive designed to end the Korean War by Christmas. Four days later his armies were retreating in the face of determined Chinese attack. It was one of the worst military reverses ever experienced by the United States. In this situation the Americans could either escalate the war or hold a line and attempt to negotiate. MacArthur advocated all out war with China. He argued that without bombing Manchuria, employing Guomindang troops, blockading the mainland and perhaps even using atomic weapons, his command would be driven from Korea. Although the administration wanted the UN to condemn China as an aggressor, it was unwilling to adopt MacArthur's strategy. Truman and Acheson wished to avoid a major war in the Far East which would leave Europe vulnerable to Soviet pressure. They were prepared to settle for a return to the status quo in Korea rather than fall into such a trap. Meanwhile they were determined to strengthen US military preparedness against the main enemy, Russia. Rearmament was accelerated, and on 16 December Truman announced that General Dwight D. Eisenhower had been appointed head of an integrated NATO command. US reinforcements were to follow. This decision marked the beginning of a major breach with MacArthur, who accorded the war he was fighting a higher priority than a hypothetical future conflict with the Soviet Union.

It was by no means certain, however, that war with China

could be avoided. The communists had to be persuaded to accept a return to the status quo in Korea, and this was unlikely as long as their forces were advancing. On 8 December Pyongyang was liberated by the NKPA (see map, p. viii). Seoul was recaptured just after New Year and a demoralized UN command driven below the 38th parallel. Until mid-January 1951 it looked as if UN troops might be pushed off · the peninsula. It was recognized in Washington that in the event of defeat, there might be little choice but to adopt MacArthur's strategy. The United States could not simply walk away from the war. Such an outcome would destroy American credibility and encourage communism everywhere. At home, where the Republicans were already seizing on the crisis to attack the foreign policy of the administration, it would be politically disastrous.

Britain reacts

British troops and journalists in Korea were dismayed by what the US Eighth Army called the 'big bug-out'. It was felt that the Americans had panicked and were retreating too quickly, breaking contact with the enemy instead of conducting a fighting withdrawal. As the British military attaché in Washington wryly remarked, the US army lacked experience of this kind of operation which had become all too familiar to the British in the early years of the Second World War. Reports from the battlefield indicated that American discipline was poor and morale weak. Amongst the British troops providing the rear-guard for Eighth Army there was a feeling of superiority border-ing on contempt for the performance of their allies, coupled with a grudging respect for the qualities of the new Chinese enemy. There was also disgust at the actions of the South Koreans who seemed more ready to massacre political prisoners than to resist the communist advance. As the ROK army collapsed there was a series of atrocities, one of which occurred on 15 December close to British troops in Seoul. The men were enraged by the killings, which included women and children.

The ROK police were driven off and further executions in the area prohibited by the British commander, who authorized the use of force if necessary.

The incident gained wide publicity at home and encouraged disillusionment with a war that was clearly going badly. The government viewed the situation with acute concern, fearing that a combination of political and military pressures might lead to American attacks on China. There was growing distrust of MacArthur, whose hostility towards Beijing and capacity for independent action were well known. A major conflict in Asia would divert military resources from Europe and the Middle East, pinning down the Americans in an area of little strategic importance. The bombing of Manchuria might even bring in the Soviet airforce and provoke a global war in which Britain would be first to suffer. Russian bombers could not reach Washington but they could hit London and US air bases in East Anglia. The government therefore wanted to confine the war to Korea and seek some solution which did not involve the United States and its allies in indefinite military commitments. It was reluctant to condemn China as an aggressor at the UN, fearing that this might clear the way to precipitate American action. At the same time Britain faced an acute dilemma. The ultimate threat to British security came from Russia, and it was difficult to contemplate a breach with the United States which might lead to the withdrawal of American support in Europe.

On 30 November Truman gave a press conference at which he implied that the use of the atomic bomb was under active consideration. Although the possibility had been discussed at the Pentagon, there were no firm plans to launch atomic warfare against China and certainly no thought of delegating authority over the bomb to MacArthur. The President may have been issuing a veiled warning to the communists not to push the United States too far. His words, however, caused consternation in London, despite an official American disclaimer. In the Commons on 30 November both sides of the house emphasized the importance of avoiding war with China. Seventy-six Labour MPs signed a statement proclaiming their unwillingness to support the government if it backed Washington in attacking

Manchuria or using the bomb. For the opposition, Churchill urged the need to stabilize the situation and underlined the supreme importance of Europe. At an emergency cabinet meeting Attlee decided it was time to fly to Washington for a summit conference with Truman. Requests for such a meeting earlier in the war had been deferred, but now the Americans were given little choice. When Attlee informed parliament of his intentions, he received an emotional response and cheers swept the House of Commons.

Attlee's flight to Washington on 3 December was intended to assert a British voice in the conduct of the war and bolster the position of the government by reassuring the public. The Prime Minister also hoped to raise the question of atomic weapons and American stockpiling of raw materials, which was having an adverse effect on the British economy and its ability to support Labour's rearmament programme. At a series of meetings with Truman and Acheson, the British delegation found broad agreement on the need to strengthen NATO and appoint an American supreme commander as soon as possible. In the Far East, the Americans conceded the importance of fighting it out within Korea and securing a ceasefire around the 38th parallel but were unprepared to pay the political price suggested by the British. Attlee emphasized that Beijing was not a slavish Soviet satellite and could be divided from Moscow. He favoured granting the communists the Chinese seat at the UN and reaching some solution to the problem of Taiwan, perhaps by means of a UN commission.

The Americans, however, were unwilling to link a ceasefire with a broader settlement. They dismissed the notion of driving a wedge in the Sino-Soviet alliance, arguing that concessions would merely reward aggression and strengthen the communist bloc. They also emphasized that China was political dynamite in the United States. The American people would not understand a policy of surrender in Asia and resistance in Europe. The raw materials question was only briefly raised and left for further study, but Attlee agreed to a large increase in the British rearmament programme, a commitment which was to cause a political crisis when it was implemented in the spring.

As for the atomic bomb, Truman stated that he would consult London before authorizing its use. His advisers, however, pointed out that this contravened the Atomic Energy Act. The final communiqué merely stated that Truman hoped he would never have to employ the bomb but would keep the Prime Minister informed, a change to which Attlee agreed 'a little sadly'.[1] Attlee did not raise the related issue of the American air bases despite the concern of the Chiefs of Staff. In theory the United States remained free to launch an atomic air offensive against Russia from Britain without seeking the approval of the British government.

UN diplomacy

On his return to London, Attlee exaggerated his achievements in averting a wider war and securing agreement on the atomic bomb. Despite his trip, doubts remained about American intentions. Although both powers agreed to seek a ceasefire through the UN, a solution proved elusive. The Chinese refused to deal with the three-man ceasefire group established by the Political Committee of the General Assembly on 12 December, and their forces continued to advance. Britain, however, was unwilling to abandon diplomatic efforts and suggested on 3 January 1951 that the group prepare a statement of principles on which a settlement might be concluded. On 11 January a supplementary report was produced which set out five principles on which a settlement might be based. These called for a Korean armistice as the prelude to a general discussion of Far Eastern questions including Taiwan and Beijing's claim to the Chinese seat at the UN. Such questions would be considered by an appropriate body, established by the General Assembly, which would include American, British, Chinese and Soviet representatives. The administration was unenthusiastic about the five principles, which threatened to provoke grave political problems at home where the Republicans were whipping up demands for the condemnation of China. As Acheson admitted, a decision was finally taken to support the plan only on the assumption that it would be rejected by Beijing. When China refused to deal on any basis other than simultaneous consideration of a Korean ceasefire and wider political issues, the Americans argued that negotiations must end. It was time for the UN to condemn China as an aggressor and consider further measures.

This demand threatened to open up the Anglo-American breach over China which the British had been anxious to avert since the beginning of the crisis. Despite the agreement to fight it out in Korea, it was by no means clear whether the Americans intended to stay, and there were rumours that an evacuation was planned. It was suspected in London that MacArthur's retreat had been too precipitate and that the general might be deliberately attempting to worsen the military situation, forcing the administration to withdraw from Korea and attack China. On 8 January Attlee wrote to Truman mentioning rumours about an evacuation and emphasizing yet again the importance of avoiding a wider war. At the same time the Chiefs of Staff despatched Air Marshal Slessor to Washington to question General Bradley. While both Truman and Bradley confirmed that the United States would not withdraw voluntarily, Bradley did not hide his pessimism about the military prospects. In fact the Pentagon doubted whether MacArthur would be able to hold a line on the peninsula and was considering options for limited retaliation against China if US forces were expelled. In these circumstances, the British were reluctant to approve any action at the UN which might give the Americans a free hand.

The government also felt domestic pressures to restrain Washington. There was widespread public concern, fuelled by the triumph of the Republican right in the recent congressional elections, that the United States was in the grip of irrational anti-communism and might drag the world over the brink. In a conversation with Dalton, Attlee agreed that the Americans were dangerously hysterical and convinced that war was inevitable. According to one report, many Labour supporters were disillusioned by ROK atrocities, alarmed by Truman's remarks about the bomb and feared that Britain had become a satellite of the United States. According to another, people were questioning the whole purpose of rearmament, which they attributed to American pressure, found the revival of Germany repugnant and required reassurance that Britain was not being pushed into conflict by the United States. It was against this background that a debate took place at the end of January 1951 about British tactics at the UN.

One group, which included junior officials such as John Strachey, the Minister of War, and Kenneth Younger, Minister of State at the Foreign Office, argued in favour of a show of independence. Britain must vote if necessary against the United States. This approach, which reflected resentment of American power and frustration at the decline of British influence within the Atlantic alliance, was supported by senior figures like Aneurin Bevan and Hugh Dalton. Others argued strongly that Britain must remain a faithful ally, restraining Washington by diplomacy rather than confrontation. According to Bevin, it would be fatal to risk a break with the Americans which would leave Britain to face the Soviet danger alone. A similar line was taken by Hugh Gaitskell, the Chancellor of the Exchequer, who argued that a break with Washington over China would have disastrous consequences. It would 'enormously strengthen the anti-European bloc in the USA ... [and] might lead to their virtually coming from Europe'.[2] These anxieties were fuelled by Acheson, who argued that failure to support the United States would have a bad effect on new American commitments to NATO which were already coming under strong attack by Republicans who favoured a policy of 'Asia first'. On 25 January, in the absence of Bevin, who was suffering from a terminal illness, the cabinet decided to vote against an American resolution condemning China. Gaitskell threatened to resign, and permanent officials of the Treasury and the Foreign Office were appalled at a decision that would have aligned Britain with the communist bloc at the UN. The following day Attlee, despite his misgivings about US policy, backed away from confrontation with Washington and persuaded his colleagues to vote for an amended resolution. This compromise was confirmed at the UN on 1 February, when Britain voted to condemn China as an aggressor and establish an additional measures committee to consider sanctions. This committee was to defer its report, however, until a good offices committee had further investigated the prospects of a political compromise.

The MacArthur problem

By the time the UN voted, the immediate military crisis had passed and it was clear that MacArthur's command would not be expelled from Korea. It was this, rather than Attlee's visit, that averted the risk of a wider war with China and opened the way to an armistice. The transformation was effected by General Matthew Ridgway, appointed to head Eighth Army just before Christmas 1950. Ridgway soon proved that it was possible not only to hold the communists without adopting MacArthur's strategy but also to push them back. By March 1951 he had recaptured Seoul, and Eighth Army was again approaching the 38th parallel. The British were reluctant to contemplate any major crossing into North Korea and felt that it was time for a new diplomatic initiative to seek an armistice. They also wanted to forestall any attempt by MacArthur to order an advance on military grounds, undermining the prospects of a compromise with China. The Americans, although doubtful that the enemy would prove receptive, were prepared to issue a declaration of war aims, emphasizing that the UN command was prepared to begin ceasefire negotiations. Although the administration emphasized that military pressure on the enemy must continue, which involved tactical crossings of the parallel, it shared the aversion of the British to a new experiment with rollback in the mountains of the north.

When MacArthur was informed about what was being considered, he sabotaged the initiative by issuing his own declaration on 24 March. This called on China to open negotiations with the UN Command or face the destruction of its ports and cities. The statement was meant to wreck the prospect of talks, appeal to American public opinion and force the administration to accept his own recipe for total victory. The British were alarmed and infuriated. As the ambassador to the UN, Gladwyn Jebb, remarked, if MacArthur thought that the UN would approve an escalation of the war 'he must be only conscious of public opinion in the Philippines, some of the banana states and the lunatic fringe of the Republican Party'.[3] When Franks raised the matter in Washington, however, the Assistant Secretary of State for Far Eastern Affairs, Dean Rusk, admitted that MacArthur had acted without authorization, but held out little hope of curbing the general. According to Rusk, any attempt to disown MacArthur would endanger the whole strategy of the administration 'including troops for Europe ... the state of Congress had never been more deplorable and difficult'.[4]

British alarm about the situation was accentuated by new military moves. At the beginning of April, the Americans, concerned by the build-up of Chinese air strength beyond the Yalu, proposed giving the UN commander authority to bomb Manchurian bases in the event of an air attack that threatened the safety of his troops. The British recoiled from this prospect, hesitating to place a blank cheque in the hands of a man like MacArthur, who might drag them into war with China at the slightest excuse. At the same time it was learned that MacArthur intended to hold a major naval demonstration off the Chinese coast. This looked suspiciously like provocation, and a protest was made to Washington. A new Anglo-American controversy was only avoided when Truman relieved MacArthur of his command on 11 April. The general had finally gone too far by criticizing the conduct of the war in a letter to a Republican Congressman, confirming the President's growing conviction that he must be fired. While British concerns may have played some part in Truman's decision, they were not decisive. The news was greeted with relief in London, but the new Foreign Secretary, Herbert Morrison, who had replaced the dying Bevin, warned his colleagues not to display their pleasure too openly. This would play into the hands of right-wing Republicans who regarded MacArthur as a martyr betrayed by an administration that was soft on Asian communism, obsessed with Europe and manipulated behind the scenes by British diplomacy.

The resignation of Aneurin Bevan

The undercurrent of discontent with the Americans came to a head just after the sacking of MacArthur, over the issue of rearmament. When Attlee visited Washington, US spokesmen emphasized the importance of showing the American people that the allies were prepared to defend themselves. Britain must spend more if it wanted US assistance. In response, on 25 January 1951 the cabinet accepted a new rearmament programme of £4,700 million over three years, a commitment that saddled the British people with 'a heavier burden of defence spending per capita . . . than was imposed in the United States'.[5] Although the Chancellor, Hugh Gaitskell, admitted the likely adverse effects on British living standards and the balance of payments, he justified the move on political grounds, arguing that it was necessary to please the Americans.

An approach that had been accepted in August 1950, however, met opposition in January 1951 when the rationality of US policy was in question. The Minister of Labour, Aneurin Bevan, who had registered concern at the earlier programme in August 1950, objected more strongly to the new burden, pointing out the excessive strain on the British economy and the danger to social services. He believed that the Soviet threat was exaggerated and called for limits on arms spending. Although Bevan accepted the cabinet decision and defended rearmament in the Commons, his opposition came to a head in the next three months and he resigned on 22 April. While the ostensible reason was the health service charges imposed in Gaitskell's budget, the underlying cause was his concern about the scale of rearmament, the sacrifice of social programmes and what he perceived as British subservience to the United States. His resignation confirmed the determination of the government to stand by rearmament as a symbol of British commitment to the Anglo-American alliance.

Compromise in the Far East

The sacking of MacArthur added fuel to the political debate in the United States. The Republicans secured a congressional hearing into his removal and attempted to capitalize on his status as a popular hero. The British were anxious to do nothing which might embarrass the administration and play into the hands of its enemies. This meant compromise in the Far East, an approach encouraged by the resignation of Bevan, which confirmed the supremacy of those who wanted accommodation in the Far East for the sake of US support in Europe. In May 1951 Britain conceded on a range of issues involving China. At the beginning of the month the government announced an embargo on rubber sales through Hong Kong. On 17 May Britain voted at the UN for a series of sanctions proposed by the additional measures committee, although these did not involve the government in any tougher action than it was already taking to deny Beijing strategic materials. At the same time Morrison announced that he did not favour conceding Taiwan to China while the Korean War lasted. As government spokesmen admitted, with China ignoring peace feelers and launching new offensives against the UN command, any other course was difficult to justify. The British agreed that the UN commander should have the authority to bomb Manchuria in the event of a sudden air attack. Morrison emphasized, however, that agreement in principle did not waive Britain's right to consultation. Washington refused to commit itself on this question and the issue was later allowed to die away, partly because the Americans might demand a similar right in the event of British military action in the Middle East where crises had broken out with both Iran and Egypt.

A compromise was also reached over the Japanese peace treaty. The Korean War had accelerated progress towards this goal, which had been delayed by bureaucratic disputes in the United States. Although Washington's new urgency was welcomed by London, Anglo-American differences soon emerged over which China should sign. The British insisted that Beijing must be invited to any peace conference. This reflected not only British contempt for the Guomindang, but also a marked fear of Japanese commercial competition. If a revived Japan were unable to resume trade relations with mainland China, its effort would be directed towards south-east Asia, where Britain wished to preserve its traditional markets. The Americans found this wholly unacceptable. It would concede legitimacy to a communist regime which had humiliated the United States in Korea, strengthen China and place Japan in a position of unhealthy economic dependence on a Soviet satellite. Moreover, the Senate would never ratify a treaty to which communist China was a party.

At the beginning of June, John Foster Dulles, who had special responsibility for the treaty, visited London for talks with Morrison which produced a compromise. Neither China would be invited to the peace conference and Japan could make its own choice after it had regained sovereignty. Although Morrison was prepared to accept, the formula was opposed by the majority of his colleagues who argued that it merely facilitated Japanese recognition of Jiang's regime on Taiwan. Morrison only won the cabinet over after a struggle during which he argued that Britain was unlikely to be offered a better deal. Further resistance would merely disrupt Anglo-American relations. It was clear that despite the deliberate ambiguity of the settlement, London had deferred to Washington. Dulles was in no doubt that the formula agreed with Morrison cleared the way to Japanese recognition of the Guomindang. By the beginning of the summer, therefore, Anglo-American differences in the Far East had been smoothed over at the price of British concessions. The process underlined American power in Asia and the decline of British influence in the region.

Conclusions

Chinese intervention ended the consensus in Britain about the Korean War and brought the Anglo-American relationship to its lowest point before Suez in 1956. It was feared in London that under pressure from the Republican right the administration might take precipitate action which would involve its allies in a wider war, perhaps of global proportions. There was particular distrust of MacArthur, who made no secret of his desire to retaliate against China and his impatience with the restraints imposed by Washington. Many doubted the ability of the administration to control him, given the charged political atmosphere in the United States. In this situation some ministers were prepared to abandon the tactic of the loyal ally pursued by Bevin since 1945. In the end, however, the government refused to go to the brink and returned to the established pattern of deferring to Washington in the Far East for the sake of US support in Europe.

Notes

1 Dean G. Acheson, *Present at the Creation* (London 1970), p. 484.
2 Philip M. Williams, *Hugh Gaitskell* (London 1982), p. 167.
3 Jebb to Foreign Office, 24 March 1951, FK1096/7 FO371/92813, Public Record Office, Kew, London.
4 Callum A. MacDonald, *Korea: The War Before Vietnam* (London 1986), p. 94.
5 Kenneth O. Morgan, *Labour in Power 1945–1951* (London 1985), p. 433.

6 Negotiations

Towards an armistice

In April/May 1951 Peng Dehuai launched two great offensives in a final attempt to drive the UN command into the sea. The Chinese were repulsed with heavy casualties and in June 1951 UN troops recrossed the 38th parallel. During the first phase of the Chinese spring offensives, the 1st Battalion, the Gloucester Regiment, was overrun at the battle of the Imjin on 22/25 April, the most serious loss suffered by the British Army during the Korean War. In the fighting the battalion inflicted heavy casualties on the Chinese 63rd Army and delayed the communist offensive, which was halted outside Seoul. The Gloucesters were awarded a US presidential unit citation but the Americans were embarrassed by the incident, which violated earlier orders against employing non-US troops as rearguards. Ridgway realized the possible political repercussions amongst the UN allies if the Americans seemed to be sacrificing their men to ensure the safety of its own and felt that the US Corps commander should have ordered the unit to retreat before it was too late. As he reiterated after the battle, 'We must not lose any battalion, certainly not another British one'.[1]

Despite the collapse of the Chinese effort south of the 38th parallel, a sustained advance into North Korea was ruled out. It was considered politically unwise to force China into a corner or to risk Soviet intervention in the war by a new attempt to eradicate the DPRK. In the spring of 1951, Moscow issued veiled warnings against any such move. Moreover, the conquest of the north would require a larger military commitment than Washington was prepared to make. An advance against communist troops fighting defensively on favourable terrain was a different prospect from defeating an enemy moving forward in the open, where the advantage lay with American firepower. Ridgway was therefore ordered to halt in the most favourable position beyond the 38th parallel, which became known as the Kansas/Wyoming Line, while the administration sought an armistice which would reduce the American military commitment in Korea. It was a decision with which Ridgway fully agreed. Unlike his predecessor MacArthur, he regarded Korea as a diversion from the main priority, preparedness against the Soviet Union.

During the MacArthur hearings in May/June 1951, which occurred while Ridgway was breaking the Chinese spring offensives, the administration defended its strategy and signalled its readiness to accept a ceasefire around the 38th parallel. At the same time diplomatic feelers were extended to Beijing and Moscow. A US official tried to make contact with the Chinese through shadowy intermediaries in the Far East, an effort which ended fruitlessly. Secret contacts between George Kennan of the State Department and Jakob Malik, the Russian ambassador at the UN, produced better results. Kennan was selected for this task because he was an expert on Russia who could be disowned if necessary, since he was on leave of absence from his post. At the second of two secret meetings in the Soviet diplomatic compound at Glen Cove, Long Island, Malik denied Russian involvement in the Korean War but indicated that Moscow favoured a settlement by direct negotiation between both sides. Three weeks later, in a radio broadcast arranged by the UN in New York, Malik called for discussions between the belligerents 'for a ceasefire and an armistice providing for mutual withdrawal from the 38th Parallel'.[2]

This was an important statement, for it did not link a Korean armistice with a wider settlement in the Far East, including Taiwan and the Chinese seat at the UN, something on which Beijing had always previously insisted. The Kremlin was probably prepared to bring pressure to bear on its Chinese ally because of the European situation. The Russian priority was to avert German rearmament, which the United States had been able to promote only because of the international tension produced by the Korean War. On 29 June, acting on instructions from Washington, Ridgway broadcast to the enemy commanders. He stated that he had been informed they might wish to discuss an armistice and proposed a meeting on a Danish hospital ship in Wonsan harbour. On 2 July Beijing radio announced that Peng Dehuai and Kim Il Sung accepted this proposal. The communists, however, wanted the talks to be held at Kaesong on the west of the peninsula just below the 38th parallel, the only area where UN troops had not yet crossed into the north. Liaison officers met at Kaesong on 8 July, and two days later talks began. The chief UN delegate was Admiral C. Turner Joy, while the communists were led by Nam Il, chief of staff of the NKPA. On the allied side the negotiations were wholly controlled by the Americans. Of the other nationalities fighting in Korea, only the ROK was represented. For information on the negotiations, Britain had to rely on State Department briefings, enquiries by its diplomats in Washington and Tokyo, and what the Joint Services Mission could learn from the Pentagon. It was considered unwise, however, to press Washington for British representation at Kaesong.

Britain and the truce talks

The ceasefire negotiations were welcomed by the government, which had long been pressing for some new declaration of UN intentions and had contemplated its own approach to Beijing. The talks not only averted the lingering threat of a wider war but also helped contain the Labour left by showing that the United States was not in the hands of extremists. At the same time it was feared that a successful ceasefire would lead to pressure from the Bevanites on the backbenches for further concessions to China, which could cause trouble in the Labour Party and also with the Americans. Morrison hoped that the armistice would be followed by an international conference on the future of Korea as the prelude to a more general settlement in the Far East. Both he and his officials, however, realized that such an outcome was unlikely in view of the US attitude towards China and the difficulty of finding a political solution even in Korea which was acceptable to both sides. As Morrison informed Acheson on 14 July, while he was hopeful that· the fighting would end, he was more doubtful about political progress and believed that a long stalemate would follow the armistice. In the meantime rearmament would improve the bargaining position of the West. Morrison was apprehensive about Syngman Rhee's proclaimed oppositon to any armistice that left Korea divided and emphasized the importance of avoiding a breakdown at Kaesong. If the talks collapsed there must be no doubt that the communists were responsible. As the US embassy in London reported, the government, plagued by domestic problems and crisis in the Middle East, was looking longingly towards the exits and had no intention of allowing Rhee to sabotage the prospects of an armistice.

The talks at Kaesong were quickly bogged down in bitter wrangling. At first, agreement proved impossible even on an agenda, and thereafter the negotiations stalled on the communist demand for a settlement along the 38th parallel. This the Americans were unwilling to concede, despite their earlier emphasis on a return to the status quo, because it would require the withdrawal of the UN command from the Kansas/ Wyoming Line and leave Seoul vulnerable to a new North Korean attack. The United States wanted a settlement along the existing battleline, establishing a demilitarized zone with the line of military contact as the median. On 22 August the communists recessed the talks, claiming that US aircraft had bombed the neutral zone established around Kaesong for the negotiations, a charge denied by the Americans. It was suspected in Washington that they wanted to bring pressure to bear on the US and its allies on the eve of the Japanese peace treaty which was to be signed in San Francisco at the beginning of September. Nevertheless the possibility remained that the Chinese had merely used the negotiations to secure a breathing space in which to rebuild their forces and intended to launch another major offensive against the UN command. The Americans had to consider their response in such a contingency.

The Acheson/Morrison meeting

The Korean situation was discussed with Morrison at the beginning of September when he visited Washington. The British were apprehensive about the stalemate at Kaesong, and the Foreign Secretary was instructed to restrain the Americans. As his brief emphasized, containment had been a success but the West must be careful not to push the Russians to the point where they opted for preventive war. This danger applied in particular to US policy in the Far East, where there was a risk that 'owing to impulsiveness or under the pressure of excitable public opinion' the Americans 'might go to unreasonable lengths'.[3] Morrison was to warn against these tendencies where necessary and emphasize the need to be constructive in relations with the USSR. He was also to pursue the issue of American air bases in Britain, where there was still no formula guaranteeing British rights, and to raise the related question of consultation about employment of the atomic bomb. The government wanted firm guarantees on these matters both to restrain the Americans and to avert political trouble at home. On Korea, Morrison was to obtain assurances that the United States would not extend the war and would keep the ROK under control. If full-scale fighting resumed, the UN command should neither advance to the Yalu nor bomb Manchuria. In the event of an armistice, there should be a new round of talks on Korea that included China. It was hoped that the Americans would not be too rigid about this and could agree to admit China to the UN and consider a wider settlement in the Far East. Morrison must have known that there was little hope of the United States agreeing to such political concessions, but he felt constrained to make a gesture towards an independent China policy.

Morrison was informed about American thinking when he met the US Secretary of State on 11 September. Acheson emphasized that if there were an armistice, the United States intended to procede with political discussions about Korea without bringing in other issues like Taiwan. He did not regard the prospects of reunification as very bright although Washington did not intend to sanctify the permanent division of the peninsula. Morrison agreed that post-armistice political discussions should be limited to Korea but was reluctant to dismiss the possibility of a more comprehensive approach to the problems of the Far East. In this connexion he mentioned British public opinion regarding China. Acheson then read an options paper produced by the Pentagon setting out possible courses of action if the truce talks failed. In such an event the Americans proposed to allow the UN command to advance to the North Korean waist beyond Pyongyang, expedite Japanese rearmament and raise additional ROK divisions. Restrictions against air attacks on the North Korean hydro-electric plants, which supplied power to both China and the DPRK, would be lifted. In the event of large-scale air attacks against UN troops, Ridgway was to carry out standing orders and inform Washington, which would, if possible, consult Britain and other UN allies before retaliating against airfields in Manchuria. At the UN, the communists would be blamed for the breakdown and the allies asked to provide additional military support. They would also be pressed to agree to an economic blockade of China.

As Acheson later recalled, British enthusiasm for the war 'had reached an irreducible minimum' and Morrison was clearly unenthusiastic about most of these options.[4] He emphasized that Britain was already facing problems in the Middle East and did not want to become further engaged against China. While there might be no alternative to retaliation against Manchuria if UN troops were bombed, nothing should be done needlessly. He quoted Bevin's advice against forcing China into the arms of Russia, a 'familiar exegesis' which merely irritated Acheson.[5] As for specific measures, Morrison agreed on the need to allow Ridgway tactical freedom but, after consulting London, asked for discussions before any advance to the Korean waist. He made it clear that the British preferred the Kansas Line to any new position further north. He foresaw no problem about increasing the ROK army but was less enthusiastic about Japanese rearmament, emphasizing the possible impact on British public opinion and also on the Soviet Union, which might become alarmed. Acheson pointed out that there was no question of using Japanese troops in Korea, at which Morrison admitted his relief. He had obviously been thinking about the Sino-Soviet pact which bound the two countries to mutual defence against the revival of Japanese imperialism. Morrison raised no problems about bombing North Korean power stations but shied away from committing more British troops to the UN command. He was unwilling to endorse economic sanctions even when Acheson stressed that these would not take the form of a naval blockade, fearing Chinese retaliation against Hong Kong.

On the atomic issue, Morrison found the Americans unwilling to make concessions. Acheson and his advisers were united in opposing any move which would establish a British right of consultation before the President could use the bomb. The negotiations were amongst the most difficult and frustrating of the visit, for Morrison lacked any real leverage to move the Americans. After the Foreign Secretary had left Washington, Franks finally secured an agreement on the air bases which made their use in an emergency 'a matter for joint decision by His Majesty's Government and the United States Government in the light of the circumstances prevailing at the time', an ambiguous formula but the best that the British could obtain.[6] The Americans believed that they had conceded little and in particular had granted Britain no veto over the employment of the atomic bomb even by the backstairs route of an agreement on the bases.

The Chancellor of the Exchequer, Gaitskell, also crossed the Atlantic in September to raise economic issues with the Americans. The Truman administration was anxious to avoid any implication that the armistice talks meant a new era of détente with the communist bloc and determined to avoid the kind of military and psychological demobilization that had occurred in 1945. While Britain agreed that the West must not let its guard down simply because of the negotiations at Kaesong, it was increasingly concerned about the impact of rearmament. In the second half of 1951 Britain experienced a severe balance of payments crisis, forcing the government to reduce the living standards of a population that had already endured three years of austerity. It was recognized that the rearmament programme agreed in January 1951 could not be sustained and that cuts were necessary despite American pressure for further increases. In talks with Acheson, Gaitskell emphasized the economic problems caused by raw materials shortages and the diversion of production from exports to the manufacture of arms. He argued that Washington must accept reductions and a greater degree of burden-sharing amongst the NATO allies to spread the costs more equitably. Although the Americans eventually agreed to review the economic capacity of the NATO countries with a view to setting more realistic rearmament targets, it came too late for the Labour government.

The return of the Conservatives

While Morrison and Gaitskell were visiting North America, Attlee called a general election. Labour performed surprisingly well, gaining its 'highest poll and the largest vote ever won by any British political party'.[7] The Conservatives, however, emerged with a narrow majority in the Commons, holding 321 seats, against 295 Labour and 6 Liberal. On 26 October Attlee resigned and it was left up to the new Prime Minister, Winston Churchill, and his Foreign Secretary, Anthony Eden, to handle the problem of Korea. As the author of the 'special relationship', Churchill was anxious to restore the Anglo-American partnership of the Second World War, which he believed had been eroded under Attlee. He realized, however, that Britain could not exercise its proper influence as long as it remained financially dependent on the United States. The economy had to be stabilized by reducing the rearmament burden inherited from Labour. This eventually led Churchill to embrace nuclear deterrence as the cheapest option, following the successful test of a British bomb in October 1952. It also made him anxious to reduce cold war tensions and to promote an armistice in Korea. At the same time, however, he was determined to play down differences with the Americans in the Far East, which he believed had been exaggerated by his predecessor. Churchill felt no sympathy for communist China and did not have to worry about splitting his party on the issue. As he remarked in January 1952, 'What Conservative in England is in favour of Chinese Communists?'[8] Churchill often displayed a nineteenth-century contempt for China, viewing options such as the bombing of Manchuria in the light of an old-fashioned punitive expedition, and warned against falling out with Washington for the sake of Beijing. While the Americans were shouldering the main burden in Korea, Britain should not act otherwise than as a loyal ally. At times Churchill implied a division of strategic responsibility, a deal by which Britain granted the United States a free hand in Asia in return for US support in the Middle East.

The new Foreign Secretary, Anthony Eden, was equally committed to the Anglo-American alliance, which he regarded as the fundamental guarantee of British security against the main enemy, the Soviet Union. Eden was no more prepared than Bevin to risk US support in Europe by emphasizing differences in the Far East. Like Churchill he held no brief for China and had been critical of the speed with which the Attlee government had recognized the communist regime. Unlike the Prime Minister, however, the Foreign Secretary was reluctant to offer the Americans a free hand in the Far East, particularly in the period before the presidential elections of November 1952, when domestic political pressures on the administration would be at their height. Eden emphasized the importance of restraining Washington, for essentially the same reasons as his Labour predecessors. An attack on China would endanger Hong Kong, commit scarce military resources to a peripheral area and risk provoking global war with the Soviet Union. It would involve political controversy at home which might endanger a government with a narrow majority and erode public support for the special relationship. It would also further burden an already strained economy. These were decisive arguments and ensured that whatever Churchill's initial impulses,

Britain would continue to pursue the diplomacy of constraint in the Korean War.

The 'greater sanctions' statement

The essential caution of the new government was soon apparent. On 25 October the armistice talks were renewed at the village of Panmunjom, a few miles to the south of Kaesong. Ridgway had insisted on the change, arguing that Kaesong was no longer a neutral site because the communists had moved up troops to surround the city. In the following month China and North Korea conceded the American demand for an armistice based on the line of military contact and not the 38th parallel. This outcome left the Kansas Line intact and assured the security of Seoul against surprise attack. It was clear, however, that further progress might be blocked by new controversies, particularly over the question of policing the ceasefire to ensure that neither side used the opportunity to strengthen its forces. Effective inspection was considered vital if the United States was to reduce its military commitments in Korea without tempting the communists to renew the war. The enemy, however, was unlikely to agree to any scheme that would satisfy the United States. In order to avoid another deadlock, the administration decided to make concessions on inspection and to seek security by threatening the Chinese with direct retaliation if they broke the armistice. Accordingly a warning was drawn up which became known as the 'greater sanctions' statement. This was to be signed by all sixteen members of the UN command and issued on the conclusion of an armistice. As a preliminary, the Americans decided to consult the British.

On 28 November, during a NATO meeting in Rome, Acheson broached the subject with Eden and asked for British support. He mentioned specific measures such as the bombing of Manchuria and a naval blockade of the Chinese coast. In the following weeks American bombing plans shifted away from Manchurian airfields towards a broader scheme intended to reinforce the effects of an economic blockade. The JCS envisaged a general campaign against the Chinese transportation system, destroying ports and railways, and mining rivers. From the beginning Eden was ready to support a step which might smooth the way to an early armistice. He realized that if Britain did not agree to the greater sanctions statement, the Americans would act unilaterally, depriving London of the right to consultation. At the same time he was unwilling to approve any course of action which might provoke retaliation against Hong Kong or risk global war. He was particularly reluctant to approve a naval blockade. The Chiefs of Staff doubted that it would be effective and raised the danger of clashes with Russian vessels using the naval base at Lushun (Port Arthur) and the harbour at Dalian (Dairen), which had been leased by China to the Soviet Union. Nor was Eden enthusiastic about bombing, although he admitted that it would cause less problems for the government than a blockade. He preferred a vague statement which avoided the appearance of an ultimatum and refused to commit Britain to specific forms of military action in advance. This represented the best chance of influencing Washington if a crisis ever arose involving the imposition of greater sanctions. By the end of December, the Americans had agreed to revised wording which was firm without being provocative. The new draft stated that if the communists breached the armistice, the consequences would be so grave that 'in all probability, it would not be possible to confine hostilities within the frontiers of Korea'.[9]

Churchill visits Washington

In early January 1952 Churchill and Eden flew to Washington for talks with Truman and Acheson on global issues. The visit was intended to evoke memories of the wartime conferences between Churchill and Roosevelt, but the British soon found that they were playing second fiddle to their more powerful ally. Churchill made no more progress than his predecessors on the question of the atomic bomb, despite his stated intention of securing full consideration from the administration on the subject, and was forced to accept the formula on US bases in Britain drawn up in the closing days of the Labour government, a formula designed to preserve American freedom of action. Like Attlee, Churchill found it expedient to exaggerate his achievement in this area on his return to London. In discussions about the Far East, the Americans emphasized their desire to limit the war and secure a viable armistice. In response to a question from Churchill about the atomic bomb, General Bradley, the chairman of the JCS, replied that the United States had no intention of using the weapon because suitable targets had not been identified. He concealed the fact that the Pentagon had conducted a series of tests in Korea the previous autumn, designed to investigate the practicality of employing atomic weapons in the field.

On tactics after an armistice, the Americans had no objection to a Korean political conference at which both Russia and China could be represented, but doubted whether it would produce results. If the armistice was breached or agreement failed to emerge at Panmunjom, they intended to bomb military targets in China and secure a UN embargo on trade. They did not believe that concessions would prise China away from the Soviet Union. As for Taiwan, the fall of the island to the communists would lead to panic throughout Asia and make it difficult to build up Japan as a bastion of Western influence. The Americans also complained about the level of trade between Hong Kong and China, producing figures collated by the Pentagon.

Churchill praised Truman's decision to intervene in Korea as a turning point in the cold war. Neither he nor Eden disputed the US view of communist China and agreed that it would be futile to seek signs of Titoism in Beijing. Nor did they advocate the surrender of Taiwan. At the same time, however, Churchill indicated his reluctance to derecognize Beijing at a crucial point in the truce talks, and Eden emphasized that the Guomindang could not be considered the legitimate government of China. The British disputed American figures on Hong Kong trade and refused to be drawn on specific measures if the armistice was breached. Churchill remarked in passing that he would not object to bombing across the Yalu if it was not for the political frontier involved. In an address to Congress, however, the Prime Minister pledged that if the truce was broken, the response would be prompt, resolute and effective. On other issues, the British emphasized the need to relieve the rearmament burden and sought American agreement on the allocation of raw materials. Churchill also emphasized the importance of dialogue with the Soviet Union. In talks on the Middle East, he received no encouragement when he angled for US support, undermining earlier ideas about trading China for Egypt and Iran.

Conclusions

Britain welcomed the armistice negotiations. By 1951 the country had become weary of the Korean War and the economic sacrifices involved in rearmament. It was hoped that a Korean ceasefire would lead to a reduction in cold war tensions which would ease the economic situation and reduce political controversy at home. Despite Churchill's rhetoric about China, these factors influenced the new Conservative government as much as its Labour predecessor. Both baulked at the prospect of extending the war and were reluctant to approve further measures against China, although recognizing that they might become inevitable if talks collapsed. There was particular opposition to any form of naval blockade, which might involve incidents with Soviet vessels or lead to retaliation against Hong Kong. Britain continued to play the part of a loyal ally, however, trying to restrain the Americans by quiet diplomacy, the approach originally established by Bevin.

Notes

1 Callum A. MacDonald, *Korea: The War Before Vietnam* (London 1986), p. 219.
2 David Rees, *Korea: The Limited War* (London 1964), p. 265.
3 MacDonald, *Korea*, p. 129.
4 Dean G. Acheson, *Present at the Creation* (London 1970), p. 538.
5 Ibid.
6 Margaret Gowing, *Independence and Deterrence: Britain and Atomic Energy 1945−52* (2 vols, London 1974), vol. 1, *Policy Making*, pp. 314−19.
7 Kenneth O. Morgan, *Labour in Power 1945−1951* (London 1985), p. 485.
8 David Carlton, *Anthony Eden* (London 1986), p. 303.
9 M. L. Dockrill, 'The Foreign Office, Anglo-American Relations and the Korean Truce Negotiations July 1951−July 1953', in James Cotton and Ian Neary (eds), *The Korean War in History* (Manchester 1989), p. 104.

7 Impasse

War and politics

Churchill returned from his American journey convinced that Britain must establish its economic and financial independence if an equal partnership with the United States was to be restored. As he explained to the cabinet, the American attitude was fundamentally affected by Britain's dependent situation and would only change when the country stood on its own two feet again, a goal which demanded reductions in the rearmament programme inherited from Labour. Despite his desire to assert the British position within the special relationship, however, Churchill faced fierce criticism from the opposition, which claimed that he had been too deferential to the Americans. It was said that the Prime Minister had approved new measures against China while in Washington, an accusation fuelled by press speculation about his address to Congress. Labour feared that such an agreement might encourage Truman to take rash action under the domestic political pressures inevitable in presidential election year. There was even more concern about what a right-wing Republican would do if elected in November. The leader of that group, Senator Taft, had made no secret of his support for the Guomindang and his desire to liberate China.

At the end of February, Labour tabled a motion in the House of Commons that amounted to a vote of censure against the Prime Minister. Churchill's instinct was to take the offensive by publishing the full range of retaliatory actions approved by the previous government. His draft reply rejected the idea of a major war with China but revealed the agreements of 1951 on retaliatory bombing of Manchurian air bases and striking certain targets on the Korean side of the Yalu if large-scale fighting resumed. It discussed the background to the 'greater sanctions' statement and emphasized that while he opposed a blockade, he had agreed before his Washington visit that in certain circumstances it might be necessary to bomb Chinese airfields, bases and lines of communication. In this he had merely followed the example of his predecessors. Churchill closed by emphasizing that divisions between Britain and the United States played into the hands of the Soviet Union, and condemning the anti-Americanism of the Labour left. The whole speech was carefully designed to humiliate the opposition and widen the breach between the Labour leadership and the Bevanites.

Churchill sent this draft to Acheson, who was visiting London. The US Secretary of State was appalled by the revelations that the Prime Minister proposed to offer. The contingency plans agreed with the British were secret and would be compromised by publicity. It did not take much imagination to work out that 'certain targets' on the Korean side of the Yalu meant the hydro-electric plants, which were the only major installations as yet unbombed in North Korea. As for the 'greater sanctions' statement, Acheson did not want this revealed until after the armistice lest it compromise the negotiations. Nor did he wish the enemy to know about the Anglo-American disagreement over economic blockade. Acheson and his assistants worked through the night at the US embassy, editing Churchill's draft into a more acceptable form, which omitted details of proposed targets and discussed greater sanctions in only the broadest terms. Although Churchill at first complained that Acheson had snatched a sword from his hand, the amended version still served his purpose by revealing that Labour had agreed to bomb China in certain circumstances, embarrassing the opposition front bench.

This episode was matched on the American side by the affair of the Yoshida letter, which was equally rooted in domestic politics. In the Anglo-American negotiations about the Japanese peace treaty, Morrison and Dulles, the US special representative, had agreed that neither China would be invited to sign and that Tokyo would be left to make its own decision after it had regained sovereignty. The problem was that the treaty required the approval of two-thirds of the US Senate, and Dulles feared that this would not be forthcoming unless the Japanese pledged in advance to deal with the Guomindang. Without such a concession the Republicans would block ratification of an agreement that the administration considered central to the US security system in the Pacific. Accordingly Dulles secured a pledge from the Japanese Prime Minister, Shigeru Yoshida, that Japan would establish relations with the regime on Taiwan and had no intention of concluding a treaty with communist China.

When the Yoshida letter was mentioned at the Washington talks, Eden argued that it contravened the Morrison—Dulles agreement. While he emphasized the dangers of a bad reaction in Japan if the West appeared to be dictating Japanese policy, his more immediate concern was probably the reaction of the opposition at home. Acheson took the view, however, that Japan had become independent when the peace treaty was signed in September 1951 and had now made its own decision. The question remained unresolved despite subsequent discussions with Dulles. The Americans concluded, however, that Eden would not object too strongly if Japan committed itself to Taiwan before the peace treaty went into effect, and published the Yoshida letter without further consultation on 16 January 1952. The timing gave the impression that Eden had approved of the move while in Washington. Labour claimed that the Americans had breached the Dulles—Morrison agreement and Acheson was forced to smooth over the issue. Eden, however, remained critical of Dulles, who he believed had been guilty of sharp practice.

The POW problem

Korea remained a topic of partisan debate in Britain as the armistice talks reached a new impasse in the spring of 1952 over the issue of prisoners of war. In theory the question was covered by Article 118 of the Geneva Convention, drawn up in 1949, which called for the automatic repatriation of *all* POWs at the end of hostilities. Although neither the DPRK nor China were signatories, both declared their intention of applying the Geneva code, Pyongyang in July 1950, Beijing not until July 1952. The United States, an original signatory, had not ratified the convention but announced at the beginning of the war that it would apply the Geneva rules. The 1949 convention, however, was not designed for conflicts like Korea, an international civil war that involved societies divided against themselves. The existence of two Koreas and two Chinas caused problems because many POWs in American hands wanted to change sides, demanding asylum in the ROK and Taiwan. In order to protect these anti-communists, the United States rejected Article 118 at Panmunjom and introduced a new concept, voluntary repatriation, which would allow each POW to choose his own fate. The American stand was based on a combination of domestic and international factors. For the Truman administration, the forcible repatriation of anti-communists was ideologically repugnant and politically impossible, particularly in an election year. Moreover, it would concede legitimacy to the DPRK and the People's Republic of China at the expense of the anti-communist regimes maintained by Washington in the ROK and Taiwan. In this respect non-forcible repatriation was a new form of rollback, designed to deny moral authority to Asian communism.

When the POW issue was raised at Panmunjom the communists rejected non-forcible repatriation. On 2 April 1952, however, a possible compromise emerged when the Chinese delegate suggested checking the POW lists to produce a total of those prepared to accept repatriation. Clearly this required sending interrogation teams to the camps in order to screen the POWs and ascertain their wishes. The communists assisted this process by providing the Americans with an amnesty statement, promising that nobody would suffer on his return home for having surrendered. It was assumed in Washington that around 116,000 of the 132,000 POWs held in compounds on Koje island would be available for exchange if the grounds for asylum were narrowly defined. The communists would probably accept such a total, opening the way to the completion of the armistice talks by the summer. In order to secure this outcome, only POWs who declared that they would forcibly resist repatriation were to be withheld from the new POW list, a subtle and short-lived shift in the American approach from voluntary to non-forcible repatriation.

A POW compromise, however, was undermined by the situation on Koje where the prisoners were bitterly divided and each compound tightly controlled by a dominant political clique. Both communists and anti-communists used terror as part of their strategy, the anti-communists who controlled the majority of the cages assisted by the South Korean guards and by Guomindang personnel imported from Taiwan to assist with propaganda programmes aimed at Chinese prisoners. The US camp command had allowed this situation to develop, partly because it lacked sufficient manpower to impose order behind the wire and partly because it sympathized with the Korean and Chinese anti-communists as ideological allies. Before screening began, the anti-communist leaders secured a majority for non-repatriation by a campaign of beatings and murder, while the communists refused to let screening teams enter their compounds. As a result, of 106,000 POWs interviewed, only 31,000 demanded repatriation. This was brought up to a total of 70,000 by counting as repatriates the communist compounds that had not been screened. The results were fatal to the prospects of an early armistice. The communists denounced screening as a fraud designed to detain prisoners for handing over to the ROK and Taiwan after the war. They could not accept without humiliation the apparent defection of over half their men in American hands. Washington, however, remained unmoved. Although the administration recognized that there had been flaws in the screening, it refused to admit coercion or Guomindang influence in the camps, since this would cast doubt on the legitimacy of the entire US stand on repatriation.

As a result the talks at Panmunjom entered a new deadlock in May 1952 on the eve of the American presidential election campaign.

Britain and the POWs

Britain watched the POW debate with acute misgivings. It was reluctant to breach the Geneva Convention, creating a precedent that might be used by the communists in future wars, and feared reprisals against British and Commonwealth prisoners in North Korea. It was also apprehensive that further delay at Panmunjom might tempt Washington to take stronger military measures against China, particularly in the tense political atmosphere of an election year. At the Foreign Office there was much scepticism about American motives. As one official remarked in January 1952, while there was an element of humanitarianism in the US approach, it was also strongly influenced by political and ideological factors. Washington, with the assistance of the Guomindang, had enjoyed some success in re-indoctrinating Chinese POWs at Koje whom it intended to repatriate to Taiwan. Britain, however, had no interest in seeing Jiang's forces strengthened at the expense of additional suffering to its own men in enemy hands.

These reservations were strengthened by what the Foreign Office learned of conditions in the camps. On 24 March a report was received from the UN commission on Korea which had recently visited Koje. This noted that the prisoners were organized by ruthless political cliques, which used terror and murder to maintain their control. The temper of individual compounds depended on whether communists or anti-communists had gained the upper hand. As one Foreign Office minute remarked: 'A deplorable state of affairs this seems . . . if one half of this should reach the ears of parliament there'd be hell to pay'.[1] On 23 April a paper was drafted for the cabinet advocating compulsory repatriation if the POW issue proved to be a breaking point in the armistice negotiations. According to the author, J.M. Addis of the Korea desk, the 'humanitarian argument, that we could not have it on our conscience to force prisoners to return to death or slavery, has been given too much importance...'.[2]

Eden sympathized with his permanent officials but was reluctant to oppose the Americans, who protested strongly when they learned about the opposition to voluntary repatriation developing within the Foreign Office. The British ambassador in Washington, Oliver Franks, left him in no doubt about the administration's determination on the issue. Eden was also under strong pressure from the Prime Minister, who considered compulsory repatriation dishonourable and emphasized the importance of standing firmly behind Washington. According to Churchill, the Americans were bearing the main burden on the battlefields of Korea and must be supported at Panmunjom. Both the Prime Minister and his Foreign Secretary were probably influenced not only by a desire to preserve good relations with Washington, but also by their experience of the Yalta agreement of 1945 by which Britain and the United States had pledged to repatriate all Soviet citizens in Western Europe at the end of the war. Many Russians had committed suicide rather than accept compulsory repatriation, and the others had faced reprisals by their own side. Eden had no wish to repeat the grisly experience, remarking in February 1952 that while the legal grounds for voluntary repatriation might be poor, this did not make him 'like the idea of sending these poor devils back to death or worse'.[3] As a result the doubts of Foreign Office officials were brushed aside and the government supported the American stand on POWs. In a letter to Attlee on 1 May, Eden emphasized that it would be 'repugnant to the sense of values of the free world to send these men home by force' and in the Commons six days later, emphasized the scrupulous fairness of the screening.[4]

The Koje riots

These statements were rapidly overtaken by events. On 8 May 1952 communist POWs on Koje kidnapped the camp commander, General Dodd, and demanded a public admission that the UNC had been guilty of brutality as the price of his release. The aim was to embarrass the Americans at Panmunjom and to cast doubts over the results of the screening. In order to save Dodd, General Colson, who assumed control at Koje, made an unauthorized statement conceding the communist charges. The whole affair infuriated the new UNC commander, General Mark Clark, who had just succeeded General Ridgway in Tokyo. Convinced that the only thing communists understood was force, Clark imposed order with a heavy hand. Combat troops, including British and Canadian battalions, were drafted onto Koje equipped with tanks, flame-throwers and tear gas. In the following weeks the anti-communists were removed from Koje, the Chinese to the island of Cheju-do and the Koreans to camps on the mainland. The communist compounds were broken up by force and the prisoners dispersed into smaller groups. There was fighting, and many POWs were killed or wounded. At Panmunjom the communists protested strongly, while in Britain the American action was condemned by the *Daily Worker* as a brutal massacre.

The Koje riots and the involvement of British troops embarrassed the government and raised doubts about Clark's judgement. Eden had defended the American position and endorsed the screening of the POWs, only to find himself faced with a crisis that raised questions about the whole basis of voluntary repatriation. In the aftermath of the Koje uprising, Labour MPs were unconvinced about the impartiality of screening, and criticized American handling of the situation. According to Attlee the fighting would never have occurred had the compounds been under British control. Although ministers continued to endorse the American stand, they felt vulnerable to Labour criticism, since their ally had not kept them fully informed. In order to reassure public opinion, deflect opposition attacks and maintain faith in the Anglo-American alliance, it was decided to send a special mission to Korea. This consisted of the Defence Minister, Lord Alexander, and the Minister of State at the Foreign Office, Selwyn Lloyd. Eden emphasized the parliamentary value of the exercise and warned the Americans that he would take it very badly if obstacles were put in the way of the visit. The State Department raised no objections. Officials, who at Franks' suggestion had been reading *Hansard*, commented that the trip would help Lloyd to answer hostile parliamentary critics.

Alexander and Lloyd met the UNC commander, Mark Clark, in Tokyo on 12 June. Alexander proposed the appointment of a British Deputy Chief of Staff to Clark's headquarters, explaining that such an officer would be able to keep the government adequately informed about military operations. Churchill clearly wanted to avoid any more surprises such as the despatch of British troops to Koje, which had left ministers exposed to parliamentary questions that they could not answer. Alexander emphasized that while Britain had only a small contingent in Korea, it was still a great power whose interests had to be taken into account. Clark raised no objections to this suggestion but was less enthusiastic when Alexander tentatively raised the possibility of British representation at Panmunjom. The Americans were determined to keep the negotiations in their own hands and were not prepared to make such a large concession to Churchill. In Korea the ministers visited the POW camps. Lloyd toured a compound for Korean non-repatriates, where he was disturbed by the presence of a strong anti-communist youth league amongst the prisoners and reports by the guards of nightly beatings behind the wire. He allowed himself to be persuaded, however, that this was a cultural rather than a political phenomenon. Koreans were simply prone to violence. He also pronounced himself satisfied with the screenings. Alexander adopted a similar view. As he reported on 17 June, the Americans had attempted little in the way of indoctrination, and the screening had been impartial and thorough. He had found no evidence of intimidation and mal-treatment except on the part of the communists, who had killed some of their fellow prisoners. These impressions were conveyed to the Canadians, who had reacted strongly to the Koje crisis, when the ministers visited Ottawa on their way home. On the basis of his personal observations, Lloyd also made a reassuring statement about the situation in the camps to Parliament on 1 July.

There is a strong suspicion that Alexander and Lloyd saw

what they wanted to see rather than risk a controversy with the Americans. The aim of their mission was to reassure the public at home and to provide the government with ammunition against opposition attacks rather than to conduct a thorough investigation. Both the ministers and the Americans understood this from the beginning. A reporter from the *Toronto Star* who accompanied Lloyd on his visit to the POW compounds recorded a radically different impression from the one conveyed to Parliament in July 1952. According to his account a 'brief investigation showed the vote [against repatriation] was unanimous because of the physical threats — often carried out — made by the [anti-communist] league members against any dissenter'.[5] As for the Chinese, the POWs had been warned by Guomindang instructors that they could either ask to go to Taiwan or remain on Koje and rot. The government was embarrassed when this report was later picked up and published in Britain by the *Daily Worker*.

While Alexander and Lloyd were in the Far East, the government was involved in a secret attempt to find a compromise on the POW problem. The process began in early May when Zhou Enlai suggested through the Indians that Britain should use its influence to break the developing impasse at Panmunjom. Although wary of a possible attempt to drive a wedge in the Anglo-American alliance, Eden was anxious to follow up this approach. The longer the war lasted, the greater the danger of escalation and British involvement in a major war with China. Eden persuaded Acheson, who was deeply suspicious of Indian diplomacy, that the opening was worth pursuing, and negotiations began with Washington on an acceptable formula to put to the Chinese. The process was complicated by the involvement of the volatile Indian ambassador in Beijing, K.M. Panikkar, who did not stick strictly to his instructions and intruded his own ideas into discussions. Nevertheless by early June his contacts with Zhou had produced a proposal that offered a way forward. This involved releasing the POWs from UNC control and handing them over to a neutral commission of four powers acceptable to both sides. Those who refused repatriation could be rescreened by the commission and Red Cross officials representing the belligerents.

Britain and the American 'air pressure' campaign

Both this secret diplomacy and the public relations exercise represented by the ministerial visit were rapidly overtaken by events. On 23 June the UN command launched a series of air attacks against the North Korean hydro-electric system including the power station at Shuifeng/Supung (Suiho) on the Yalu, the largest generating station in the Far East (see map, p. viii). Shuifeng/Supung supplied electricity to China and the Soviet Union as well as to North Korea and had always been regarded as a politically sensitive target for this reason. The raids represented an intensification of air warfare by the Americans, designed to force the communists to terms at Panmunjom without incurring the heavy US casualties involved in ground offensives. The Shuifeng/Supung attack caused a furor in Britain. The opposition denounced the American action as an escalation of the war, about which Britain had not been consulted. As Attlee pointed out on 25 June, the raid could not have been carried out without extensive preparations, which must have been taking place while Alexander and Lloyd were in Korea, yet they had not been informed about what the Pentagon hailed as the biggest single air attack of the war. There was no point in sending high-ranking ministers to the Far East if the Americans avoided full and frank discussion with them. While he agreed that Washington must control UN military operations, it did not mean that Britain should have no say in the conduct of the war. It was time for the government to assert British influence.

The government defended the bombing as a routine military operation and denied that a change of policy had occurred. Privately, however, ministers were furious about an American action which fuelled opposition criticism and endangered the prospects of a compromise with China on the POW question. On 24 June, at a meeting in Washington, Lloyd complained that the timing of the raids was inappropriate and pointed out the domestic political consequences in Britain, where people were worried about the conduct of a war in which their country seemed to lack an appropriate voice. If Churchill had been consulted he would probably have approved, but instead the

Prime Minister had been placed in an embarrassing situation. Lloyd emphasized the necessity for Allied consultation on military decisions with a high political content and complained about the tendency of the Pentagon to ignore Britain. The following day an embassy official complained about the ammunition the Americans had supplied to the Bevanites. If their objective was to overthrow the government, they were going about it in the right way. Eden himself pleaded with Acheson for no more surprises along the lines of Shuifeng/Supung.

It is unclear why the United States did not inform its ally about the raids in advance. Britain had agreed to the bombing of Shuifeng/Supung during the Morrison/Acheson discussions of September 1951, but only in the event of a breakdown in the truce negotiations. Clark's claim that the operation had not been approved by Washington while the British ministers were in Korea was somewhat disingenuous, since he could easily have mentioned that an escalation of the air war was under consideration. The real reason for American secrecy was probably doubt about British security following the defection of the two diplomats, Guy Burgess and Donald MacLean, to Moscow in May 1951. Shuifeng was within easy reach of the main Chinese air base at Dandong, and the attackers might have suffered heavy casualties had the communists been forewarned. It may also have been suspected in Washington that the British would object to the operation if they were informed in advance, encouraging a decision to present London with a *fait accompli*.

The crisis was defused when Washington agreed to the appointment of a British deputy to Mark Clark on 27 June, and Acheson, who was visiting London, informed a gathering of MPs in Westminster Hall that a mistake had been made and that Britain should have been consulted about the bombing of Shuifeng. He trod a careful line in his speech between conciliating his immediate audience and offering ammunition to the Republicans at home who had always believed that Acheson's policy was too deferential to London. While these concessions relieved the immediate political pressure on the government, an undercurrent of dissatisfaction with American handling of the Korean War remained. As for the secret contacts with China, they collapsed in the wake of the raids, which were condemned by Beijing as a new form of gunboat diplomacy. It was unclear whether or not Zhou had been on the verge of offering substantial concessions as Nehru claimed, but the Foreign Office considered the bombing at best ill-timed since the Chinese would not want to appear to weaken under American military pressure.

Conclusions

Eden and many of his officials had strong reservations about the US position on POWs, which proved to be the ultimate sticking point in the negotiations at Panmunjom, but they were not supported by Churchill, who backed the Americans on both moral and political grounds. Britain in any case had little choice but to follow the US lead. The alternative was a bitter argument with Washington, which was likely to exhaust British influence to little purpose. Eden thus swallowed his misgivings and defended the American stand. His attempt to reassure the British public and hold the line in Parliament, however, was quickly threatened by the Koje uprising, which raised inevitable questions about the real situation in the camps. In response Eden tried to demonstrate British influence by sending Alexander and Lloyd to the Far East, but the American decision to escalate the air war in June 1952 plunged the government into further controversy in the House of Commons. Once again Eden was forced to defend an action about which he had strong private doubts. In the following months he was to redouble his efforts to restrain the Americans, while attempting to contain the opposition at home. At the same time he was to renew the attempt to find a compromise with Beijing through the Indians, an attempt which was to cause new friction with Washington in the autumn of 1952.

Notes

1 Callum A. MacDonald, 'Heroes Behind Barbed Wire: The US, Britain and the POW Issue in the Korean War', in James Cotton and Ian Neary (eds), *The Korean War in History* (Manchester 1989), p. 145.
2 M. L. Dockrill, 'The Foreign Office, Anglo-American Relations and the Korean Truce Negotiations July 1951–July 1953', in Cotton and Neary (eds), *The Korean War in History*, p. 106.
3 MacDonald, 'Heroes Behind Barbed Wire', p. 145.
4 Dockrill, 'The Foreign Office, Anglo-American Relations and the Korean Truce Negotiations', in Cotton and Neary (eds), *The Korean War in History*, p. 107.
5 MacDonald, 'Heroes Behind Barbed Wire', p. 146.

8 Armistice

Controversy at the UN

In the closing months of the Truman administration, Britain remained concerned about American tactics on both the military and diplomatic fronts. With the truce talks still deadlocked over the POW issue, the United States intensified the bombing of North Korea in an attempt to force the communists to terms before the presidential elections of November 1952. Britain had long been sensitive to the impact of American bombing on both domestic and Asian opinion. As early as August 1951 the Labour government had asked Washington about Chinese claims of indiscriminate attacks on population centres. By the following year area raids on cities like Pyongyang, employing napalm as well as high explosives, had become routine. In one raid on the North Korean capital 2,300 gallons of napalm were dropped. These attacks were denounced by the *Daily Worker*, which had been condemning American bombing ever since 1950, and by communist sympathizers such as Monica Felton in her pamphlet *What I Saw In Korea*. The communist campaign also spread charges launched by the Chinese and North Koreans in February 1952 claiming that the United States was waging biological warfare against the civilian population by dropping infected insects behind the lines.

The government was concerned about the possible impact of the germ warfare charges on Asian and particularly Indian opinion. In Britain itself, the communist claims gained little credence although they roused the ire of Tory backbenchers against those who endorsed them, such as Hewlett Johnson, the so-called 'Red Dean of Canterbury'. The conventional bombing of the North, however, was a different matter and by 1952 was engaging the attention of respectable sectors of opinion. The indiscriminate use of napalm was considered particularly offensive. The Archbishop of York, the Methodist Church conference and the Free Church of Scotland all questioned the employment of napalm in Korea. Churchill was also disturbed by the use of the weapon against population centres. The British did not pursue the issue, however, when it became clear that the Americans did not welcome questions about their conduct of the air war.

By that stage London and Washington were involved in a larger dispute over repatriation of POWs, which ended the British relationship with the outgoing Truman administration on a sour note. The scene was the autumn session of the UN General Assembly, which was held against a background of stalemate at Panmunjom, where the Americans had indefinitely recessed the talks on 8 October. Eden went to the General Assembly determined not to be stampeded into hasty action against China, particularly in the form of an economic blockade. He continued to look for some compromise that would end the war and avert the risk of escalation under a new administration, an escalation that he suspected would be welcomed by the UNC commander General Clark and hawks in the Pentagon. In pursuit of this aim, Eden endorsed the solution proposed by the Indian delegate, Krishna Menon, who claimed to be in touch with Beijing. Menon's scheme, which bore traces of the earlier formula discussed by Zhou and Panikkar, called for non-repatriate POWs to be handed over to a neutral commission after the armistice, which would hold the prisoners for an indefinite period while all means short of force were used to persuade them to return home.

The Menon plan, which was also supported by the Canadian President of the General Assembly, Lester Pearson, ran into bitter opposition from Acheson, who had come to the meeting determined to mobilize international support behind the American stand at Panmunjom. Acheson despised the Indians as appeasers and accused the British and Canadians of joining them in a cabal behind his back. He condemned the Indian scheme as forcible repatriation, since the POWs faced indefinite detention unless they agreed to return home. Acheson attempted to convert the issue into a vote of confidence in American leadership, hinting that unless Britain fell into line, the United States might be forced to reconsider its commitments to NATO, an echo of his approach during 'the earlier UN debate over the condemnation of China in January 1951. Eden, however, refused to abandon the Menon plan, concentrating instead on amending it in ways that met American objections. Despite various concessions, including setting a definite time limit on the detention of POWs by the neutral commission, Acheson remained adamant. Eden attributed his continuing opposition to the defeat of the Democrats in the presidential elections, and Acheson's reaction to years of McCarthyite attacks. His last act as Secretary of State was not going to be one that could be condemned as appeasement of communism. Acheson only endorsed the amended Menon plan after it had been attacked by the Russians, narrowly averting a public Anglo-American quarrel. Although the General Assembly resolution endorsing the Menon plan was rejected by China and the DPRK in December 1952, it was later to provide the framework for a solution to the POW problem.

Changing the guard — Britain and the Eisenhower administration

On 5 November 1952 the US presidential election was won by the Republican candidate, Dwight D. Eisenhower. The nomination of Eisenhower had been a considerable relief to Britain, which had feared the selection of a right-winger like Taft, who had made no secret of his desire to roll back communism in the Far East. By contrast Eisenhower was a familiar ally from the days of the Second World War, who had been closely associated with the policies of the Truman administration. In May 1952, when he resigned his post as NATO commander to run in the election, Eisenhower was given a farewell dinner by Churchill at which he emphasized his commitment to the special relationship. In the course of the campaign, however, Eisenhower made his peace with the right, flirting with the concept of rollback (the liberation of the Soviet satellites from communism), appearing on a platform with McCarthy, and attacking the administration's handling of the Korean War. On the evening of Eisenhower's election victory, Churchill confessed to unease about the prospect of a Republican in the White House and later speculated that it might have been better if the Democratic candidate, Adlai Stevenson, had won. As for Eisenhower's choice as Secretary of State, John Foster Dulles, Churchill regarded him as 'a stupid man and could hardly stand the sight of him'.[1] The Prime Minister's view was encouraged by Dulles' association with the doctrine of liberation and by the tough ideological line he adopted at his Senate confirmation hearings in January 1953, when he emphasized the irreconcilable conflict between capitalism and communism. Nor was Dulles popular with the Foreign Office, despite giving private reassurances about US policy. Although Eden may later have exaggerated his personal dislike of Acheson's successor, he informed Churchill in November 1952 that Dulles would not have been his choice for the State Department.

In November 1952 Churchill informed his Principal Private Secretary, John Colville, of his concern about the political outcome in the United States, remarking that Eisenhower's triumph made war much more likely. The Americans had successfully tested their first hydrogen bomb in September 1952, and Churchill apparently feared that Washington might be tempted to use the new weapon to launch a pre-emptive strike against the Soviet Union. This would put Britain with its US air bases in the front line. The prospect encouraged an ambition that Churchill had held since his period in opposition, to promote a summit conference that would reduce international tension and the risk of war. Such an outcome would confirm his reputation as a world statesman and Britain's status as a great power which had slipped since the wartime meetings of the Big Three at Tehran, Yalta and Potsdam. Churchill's enthusiasm for a summit was not shared by Eden, but he was to seize his opportunity the following spring when the Foreign Secretary was incapacitated by the illness that dogged his later career.

The British decided to use their influence to avert hasty decisions by the new administration under pressure from the right wing and military hawks such as General Clark, who hoped to convert Republican election rhetoric about rolling back communism into reality. Eden believed that the only safe course was to continue the static war while keeping casualties low. On 11 November, in a speech at the Lord Mayor's banquet, Churchill pledged British cooperation with Eisenhower but warned against escalation in Korea, which would only play into Soviet hands. He emphasized his desire to bring the conflict to a speedy end if it could be done without repatriating POWs against their will. In January 1953 the Prime Minister visited the United States to take his farewell of the Truman administration and to assert his influence with its successor. Eisenhower had just returned from an inspection trip to Korea and it was considered important to neutralize any arguments put forward by Clark in favour of widening the war. During his talks with the President-elect and Dulles, Churchill urged caution on issues like Korea. When Dulles raised the possibility of unleashing Jiang, withdrawing British recognition from Beijing and instituting an economic blockade of the Chinese mainland, he received no encouragement. As Colville emphasized, such actions would not end the war and would only exacerbate public opinion in Britain.

Despite these pre-emptive moves, the relationship with the new administration started badly. On 2 February 1953 Eisenhower announced that the US 7th fleet would no longer be used to neutralize the Taiwan straits, apparently clearing the way for a Guomindang invasion of the mainland, a move long advocated by the Republican right. In fact the announcement was part of a strategy of psychological pressure against Beijing, and Jiang was privately warned against any such move. Eden, however, reacted badly to the announcement, which ignored British interests, alarmed the Indians and complicated his problems with the opposition. On 3 February he informed the Commons that the American move would have unfortunate political repercussions without compensating military advantages. Dulles was quickly despatched across the Atlantic to reassure London that the administration had no intention of unleashing Jiang, but an undercurrent of concern remained that Eisenhower might take dramatic steps to appease the Republican right wing and end a frustrating war. In this situation, Eden renewed his effort to break the deadlock at the truce talks. In January 1953, after a meeting with the President of the International Red Cross, he proposed an exchange of sick and wounded POWs. The Americans agreed and on 22 February Clark raised the question through his liaison officers at Panmunjom. At the same time Eden approached the Russians and asked them to use their influence to secure the release of civilian internees, including the British minister to Seoul, captured in June 1950 when the city fell to the NKPA. These initiatives, however, produced no immediate results.

At the beginning of March Eden visited Washington, where he had talks with Dulles. The new Secretary of State made it clear that although no final decisions had yet been made, the Eisenhower administration was determined to disengage from Korea. Dulles emphasized that in default of an armistice further military moves might be required before this proved possible, including bombing Manchuria and a ground advance to the North Korean waist. This line could then be fortified and turned over to the ROK which would be economically strengthened by the incorporation of the new territory. Only the rump of the DPRK would be left to the communists. Eden did not object to extended bombing but asked that the United States launch no major offensives without consulting Britain. He also warned Dulles that London would oppose anything like a naval blockade of China, which might provoke a clash with the Soviet Union. Dulles was less than frank with Eden during their conversation. As early as February 1953 Eisenhower had speculated about using atomic weapons to break the military deadlock, and in the spring Pentagon planners began working on a series of options along such lines. It was realized from the beginning that such a move would cause grave problems with the British, but Eisenhower's political credibility depended on ending the war. He was to use the hint that atomic warfare was under consideration to pressure Beijing into accepting an armistice that incorporated American views on the repatriation of POWs. Whether Eisenhower would in fact have employed atomic weapons in Korea and Manchuria if the stalemate had continued at Panmunjom must remain an open question.

Breakthrough – the death of Stalin

On 5 March 1953, while Eden was in Washington, Stalin died. This event had a dramatic effect on the prospects of a truce in Korea, as his successors attempted to reduce tension with the West. On 15 March the new Soviet leader, Georgi Malenkov, announced that there were no disputes between Russia and the United States that could not be solved by negotiation. What this meant in the Far East was revealed when Zhou Enlai returned from Stalin's funeral. On 28 March the communists agreed to the UNC proposal for an exchange of sick and wounded POWs. Two days later the Chinese Foreign Minister announced on Beijing radio that he was willing to have all non-repatriate POWs turned over to a neutral state so as to ensure a just solution to the question of their repatriation. This statement was echoed by Kim Il Sung and publicly endorsed by the Russians. The communists made it clear that they regarded the exchange of sick and wounded as an opportunity to resume the armistice talks, recessed by the Americans since October 1952. As further evidence of goodwill, the DPRK released the civilian internees on 8 April and repatriated them via Moscow. In this situation, the British pressed the Americans to return to Panmunjom as quickly as possible. According to Churchill it would be a pity if a sudden frost nipped spring in the bud. The Prime Minister believed that in the new atmosphere created by the death of Stalin, an opportunity existed not only to conclude a Korean armistice but also to launch his own plan for a summit meeting, which he had held in abeyance as long as the Soviet dictator lived.

Eisenhower was more cautious about the prospects in Korea

and insisted on progress in the exchange of sick and wounded POWs as evidence of communist good faith. As for Churchill's summit plans, the President was unencouraging. He was careful, however, not to put impossible preconditions on a Korean armistice in his public response to communist statements, and the talks at Panmunjom were resumed on 26 April 1953. After a series of wrangles, the chief communist delegate, Nam Il, made a new proposal on 7 May, suggesting that after the armistice non-repatriate POWs should be handed over to a neutral commission consisting of Sweden, Switzerland, Poland, Czechoslovakia and India. The commission would hold non-repatriates for four months while they were given 'explanations' by their own side to persuade them to return home. The fate of those remaining after this period would be settled by the political conference that was to be held under the terms of the truce agreement. This proposal was close to the UN resolution of December 1952 and represented a considerable concession by the communists.

The United States, however, adopted a tough attitude towards the plan, insisting that it failed to offer the non-repatriates speedy liberation at the end of the war. Unless the prisoners accepted communist explanations and returned home, they faced the prospect of indefinite detention. Nor did the administration trust the Indians, fearing that they would vote with Czechoslovakia and Poland, providing the communists with a majority on the commission. The Americans also had to consider their relations with the ROK. Rhee had hoped that the Republicans would support the total liberation of his country and was bitterly disappointed when Eisenhower resumed the discussions at Panmunjom. He threatened to withdraw ROK troops from the UN command rather than accept a settlement which left Korea divided, and objected strongly to the idea of handing over the Korean non-repatriates to a neutral commission. Since his soldiers provided most of the guards for the POW camps he had the power to veto any such move.

On 13 May the Americans responded to the communist proposal with a plan of their own which reflected their determination to guarantee asylum to the non-repatriates and avoid a quarrel with Rhee. They accepted the principle of a neutral commission but insisted that after sixty days it must release the remaining prisoners and disband. India alone was to provide the guard force in order to prevent dirty tricks by the Czechs and the Poles. The Korean non-repatriates were to be freed on the conclusion of the armistice, and only the Chinese were to be handed over to the commission. The communists denounced this as a step backwards and recessed the talks for four days. According to the New China News Agency, the prospects of a truce depended on a speedy resolution of the points at issue.

The apparent impasse at Panmunjom caused immense disquiet in Britain. It seemed incredible that Washington would risk a breakdown over the details of POW repatriation when the armistice had been largely agreed and the communists had gone so far towards accepting the position agreed by the UN in December 1952. There was a strong feeling that American handling of the negotiations had been inept and inflexible, deferring to pressure from the Republican right wing and Syngman Rhee. In the Commons on 13 May, Attlee went so far as to ask if Eisenhower or McCarthy was in charge of US foreign policy. Churchill, warned by Nehru that the Chinese were considering withdrawing their concessions, protested to Washington. From the British point of view as long as the principle of non-forcible repatriation was maintained the details did not matter. It was better to sacrifice a few individuals than to put at risk the prospect of an armistice. This was all the more important because the collapse of negotiations would destroy the new atmosphere created by the death of Stalin and undermine Churchill's wider plans. In a Commons speech on 11 May, the Prime Minister openly expressed his desire for a summit conference with Russia.

Rhee takes a hand

The Eisenhower administration, besieged by its UN allies and anxious to secure an armistice rather than escalate the war, proposed a compromise. It conceded that the neutral commission should take custody of all non-repatriate POWs, Chinese as well as Koreans, but insisted that those who refused to return home despite explanations must be freed after a fixed period. On 26 May this plan was formally tabled at Panmunjom as the final and irrevocable position of the UN command and accepted by the communists nine days later. As the belligerents moved towards finalizing the armistice, however, Syngman Rhee intervened, creating a new crisis behind the front. In the following weeks it was sometimes difficult to remember that the real enemy was in Pyongyang and Beijing rather than in the lodgings of the ROK President at Pusan. Rhee was furious at the change in the American negotiating position about which he was informed only at the last minute and immediately withdrew his representative at Panmunjom. He threatened to fight on alone even at the risk of national suicide and on 18 June ordered ROK guards to free the prisoners in the camps for Korean non-repatriates. This action raised questions about the subordination of ROK forces to the UN command and undermined the POW compromise already agreed with the communists. It jeopardized the entire armistice, since the fighting could not be ended without the consent of Rhee, whose army now held two-thirds of the front.

The British were furious at Rhee's sabotage. There was little sympathy in London for Korean nationalism or for Rhee personally, who had always been an embarrassment, particularly after the atrocities committed by his security forces in the first months of the fighting. In 1952 he had caused further problems by undermining the public image of the war maintained by the UN allies. In an attempt to guarantee re-election he had declared martial law in Pusan and arrested opposition congressmen, an action that had earned him a British rebuke and had led the Americans to consider the possibility of a military coup. His latest move was considered the last straw. As Churchill complained on 3 July: 'If I were in charge I would withdraw the United Nations troops to the coast and leave Syngman Rhee to the Chinese ... Korea does not really matter now. I'd never heard of the bloody place until I was seventy-four'.[2] From the Prime Minister's point of view the war had served its purpose by stimulating American rearmament, allowing the West an opportunity to negotiate with the Russians from a position of strength. The Korean leader must not be allowed to damage this prospect. In a personal telegram to Eisenhower, Churchill went so far as to propose the arrest or removal of Rhee by the UN command. His rage was shared by many Foreign Office officials. According to Gladwyn Jebb, the British ambassador to the UN, it was intolerable that 'this elderly brigand ... should presume to enrol the Americans, ourselves and the whole of the Western World in a crusade against Communism'.[3] As both Churchill and the Foreign Office realized, however, everything depended on the Americans, who argued that the solution must be left up to them.

Rhee's attempts to sabotage the armistice caused a new controversy between London and Washington over the 'greater sanctions' statement agreed at the end of 1951. British reluctance on the issue was evident as early as May 1953 when the talks were resumed at Panmunjom, probably because Churchill did not want to spoil the new international atmosphere created by the death of Stalin or risk a parliamentary row with the Labour opposition by appearing too belligerent. The Americans made it clear that they would react badly if Britain reneged. The 'greater sanctions' statement was fundamental to the armistice, since without it the United States would have been much tougher on issues like inspection and airfield reconstruction. Rhee's defiance gave London new reasons for concern, which were shared by the rest of the UN allies. As the British ambassador informed Dulles, the language of the statement might no longer be appropriate in view of the danger that the ROK rather than the communists would breach the armistice. Britain had no intention of being dragged into a major war with China for the sake of Syngman Rhee.

While the debate on the 'greater sanctions' statement was continuing, the United States was trying to persuade Rhee to accept an armistice. It was a frustrating experience, since he proved stubborn and continually evaded agreement. By the middle of July, however, the South Korean leader, to the relief of Washington and London, had finally backed away from the brink. His decision was probably encouraged by sustained Chinese attacks against ROK troops, which proved the impossibility of South Korea fighting successfully on its own. While Rhee still refused to sign an armistice, he agreed not to oppose one, an outcome that the Americans accepted as better than nothing. Rhee's tactics won considerable concessions for the ROK, including a military security treaty and a pledge of post-war US economic assistance.

With Rhee's objections neutralized, an armistice agreement was signed at Panmunjom on 27 July, which ended the fighting along a demarcation line based on the existing front. The following day Britain and the other UN allies initialled the 'greater sanctions' statement. It was not issued immediately as originally planned, but incorporated into Clark's final report to the UN, which was not published until 7 August 1953. This avoided the appearance of an open threat, which might have encouraged Rhee and raised doubts in Asia about the real commitment of the UN to a ceasefire. For the Churchill government it had the added attraction of appearing during the parliamentary recess when the political repercussions could be minimized. Churchill was careful to emphasize that the statement did not concede the Americans a free hand in the event of future trouble with Beijing. Greater sanctions did not mean British approval for a general war with China or a global war involving both China and the Soviet Union. The Korean War thus ended as it had begun, with Britain warning against the dangers of a major conflict in the Far East.

Conclusions

In the final year of the war the British redoubled their efforts to break the impasse in Korea. It was feared that the alternative would be an escalation in the fighting and perhaps a wider war, a fear fuelled by the triumph of the Republicans in the presidential elections and the rhetoric of liberation sometimes employed by officials like Dulles. British efforts, however, came to nothing until the death of Stalin in March 1953, which broke the deadlock at Panmunjom. In the following weeks the government urged the importance of flexibility on the controversial

POW issue and reacted angrily to Rhee's attempts to sabotage the armistice. When the fighting ended, the Churchill government, like its Labour predecessor, hoped for progress towards a political settlement in the Far East although recognizing the difficulties that lay in the way. It proved impossible, however, to take even the first step, an agreement on Korea. Talks on reunification at the Geneva conference in 1954 ended in deadlock and Korea remained divided. Nor were the Americans persuaded of the need to do business with China. The Eisenhower administration, like its predecessor, continued to believe that the best way to foster a Sino-Soviet split was to maintain pressure on Beijing. The following years were marked by crises first over Indo-China and then over Taiwan and the offshore islands of Jirmen (Quemoy) and Masu (Matsu), which raised anew British fears of a major war in the Far East.

Notes

1 Stephen E. Ambrose, *Eisenhower: the President 1952–1969* (New York 1984), p. 21.
2 Callum A. MacDonald, *Korea: The War Before Vietnam* (London 1986), p. 187.
3 M.L. Dockrill, 'The Foreign Office, Anglo-American Relations and the Korean Truce Negotiations July 1951–July 1953', in James Cotton and Ian Neary (eds), *The Korean War in History* (Manchester 1989), p. 113.

9 Conclusions

The Korean War and the limits of influence

The Korean conflict, although described as a limited 'police action', had global consequences. It militarized the cold war and raised international tension to new heights. Within months of the North Korean attack, Washington had proposed the integration of West German troops into NATO and embarked upon a massive rearmament programme designed to put the United States and its allies in a position to fight and win a global war with Russia by 1954. When China intervened in Korea at the end of 1950 it seemed as if the world would be plunged into a wider war even earlier. President Truman proclaimed a state of national emergency and American rearmament was accelerated. Britain was caught up in these events as London attempted to follow Washington's lead. Although Korea was initially a popular cause, the public mood rapidly shifted as victory receded and the Treasury attempted to budget for a rearmament programme beyond the country's resources. Economically the effects were disastrous. Recovery was delayed and Britain entered a new balance of payments crisis in 1951. The political consequences were equally dramatic, provoking dissension in the Labour Party, the resignation of Aneurin Bevan and the fatal weakening of an already tired government. Six months later Attlee was narrowly defeated by the Conservatives under Winston Churchill.

Korea also produced friction in the Anglo-American alliance, which reached its lowest point before Suez in the winter of

1950/51. As the country faced the possibility of global atomic war, there were increasing reservations about US policy. American public opinion appeared to be in the grip of the mindless anti-communism symbolized by Senator Joe McCarthy, and the feeling grew that Britain must assert its position within the 'special relationship'. The task was no longer to steer the United States away from isolationism, but to contain American power. Although the immediate crisis passed in the spring of 1951, the fear that the United States might plunge its allies into a wider war by some ill-considered action persisted until the armistice. In this situation, Britain looked longingly towards the exits. Indeed by 1953 Winston Churchill hoped that a Korean ceasefire would lead to broader negotiations between the blocs, reducing international tension and the risk of global war.

In pursuing the diplomacy of constraint, Britain came up against the inequalities of power within the 'special relationship'. Both Attlee and his successor, Churchill, might demand 'a place on the bridge within reach of the wheel' but they were to be disappointed.[1] Neither was able to regain a veto over American use of the atomic bomb, an issue which became urgent after China intervened, and despite their best efforts achieved only an ambiguous formula covering US air bases in Britain. Both found it expedient to exaggerate what they had gained in this area. There is no evidence that British pressure prevented the Americans from adopting any course which they might otherwise have taken in the Far East. In particular it is a myth that Attlee's famous visit to Washington in December 1950 saved the world from a wider war. It was the stabilization of the military situation and not Attlee's intervention which kept the Korean War within bounds. British diplomacy was frustrated by the realities of power. It was dangerous to emphasize Anglo-American differences in the Far East because Britain ultimately depended on the United States to contain the Russians in Europe and provide financial assistance for rearmament. As for Churchill's hope of securing American backing in the Middle East in return for acting as a loyal ally in Asia, he was to be disappointed. Neither Truman nor Eisenhower was in the business of propping up the threatened British position in Iran or Egypt, emphasizing instead the need to conciliate emerging nationalist movements. When the Americans finally moved in the case of Iran, it was not for the sake of Britain but to promote their own interests. It was thus London and not Washington which made compromises for the sake of the 'special relationship'. Korea exposed British illusions about guiding the American colossus and revealed, well before Suez in 1956, the shift towards US hegemony within the Atlantic alliance.

Note

1 *The Economist*, 2 February 1952, pp. 218–19.

Dramatis Personae

ACHESON, DEAN. US Secretary of State, January 1949–January 1953

ALEXANDER, LORD. British general. Minister of Defence, October 1951–October 1954

ATTLEE, CLEMENT. Prime Minister, July 1945–October 1951

BEVAN, ANEURIN. Minister of Health, July 1945–January 1951. Minister of Labour and National Service, January 1951–April 1951

BEVIN, ERNEST. Foreign Secretary, July 1945–March 1951

BRADLEY, OMAR. US General. Chairman of JCS 1949–1953

CHURCHILL, WINSTON. Prime Minister, October 1951–April 1955

CLARK, MARK. US General. Head of UN Command and US Far East Command, May 1952–July 1953

DALTON, HUGH. Minister of Town and Country Planning, February 1950–October 1951

DULLES, JOHN FOSTER. US Secretary of State, January 1953–April 1959

EDEN, ANTHONY. Foreign Secretary, October 1951–April 1955

FRANKS, OLIVER. British ambassador to Washington, 1948–1952

GAITSKELL, HUGH. Chancellor of the Exchequer, October 1950–October 1951

KIM IL SUNG. North Korean leader

MACARTHUR, DOUGLAS. US General. Headed occupation of Japan and US Far East Command. Head of UN Command, July 1950–April 1951

MORRISON, HERBERT. Foreign Secretary, March 1951—October 1951

NEHRU, JAWAHARLAL. Indian leader

PANIKKAR, KAVALAM. Indian ambassador in Beijing

PENG, DEHUAI. Chinese general. Commander of Chinese People's Volunteers in Korea

RHEE, SYNGMAN. South Korean leader

RIDGWAY, MATTHEW. Commander of Eighth Army in Korea, December 1950—April 1951. Head of UN Command and US Far East Command, April 1951—May 1952

SHINWELL, EMMANUEL. Minister of Defence, February 1950—October 1951

ZHOU ENLAI. Chinese Foreign Minister

Outline Chronology

1945

14 August	Japan surrenders
15 August	US and Soviet Union agree to temporary division of Korea at 38th parallel
27 December	Moscow Foreign Ministers' Conference (Britain, Russia, United States) agrees plan for Korean independence

1946

8 May	US—Soviet talks on Korean reunification end in deadlock

1947

12 March	Proclamation of Truman Doctrine
17 September	US takes Korean problem to United Nations when new round of talks with Russia ends in deadlock

1948

15 August	Republic of Korea (South Korea) inaugurated in Seoul under Syngman Rhee after separate elections in South sponsored by UN

| 9 September | Democratic People's Republic of Korea (North Korea) inaugurated in Pyongyang under Kim Il Sung |
| 25 December | Russian troops withdraw from North Korea |

1949

| 30 June | US troops withdraw from South Korea |

1950

6 January	Britain recognizes People's Republic of China
25 June	North Korean forces cross 38th parallel
25 June	UN Security Council calls for North Korean withdrawal
27 June	UN Security Council calls for members to render military assistance to ROK (South Korea)
28 June	Britain commits naval units to Korea
7 July	UN Command established under General MacArthur
14 July	Britain tightens controls on exports to China
25 July	Britain agrees to raise 29th Brigade for Korea (arrives mid-November)
4 August	NKPA drives UN Command into Pusan perimeter
17 August	Britain commits 27th Brigade to Korea from Hong Kong (arrives 28 August)
12 September	Government announces £3,600 million rearmament programme over next three years
15 September	MacArthur's landing at Inchon outflanks NKPA and changes course of war
2 October	Zhou threatens Chinese intervention if US troops cross 38th parallel
7 October	UN General Assembly passes resolution on reunification of Korea

9 October	US troops cross 38th parallel
31 October–2 November	First clashes with Chinese troops in North Korea
13 November	Britain proposes halting UN advance and establishment of demilitarized zone south of Yalu River
24 November	MacArthur launches 'final offensive'
26 November– 24 December	Chinese forces halt UN advance and force retreat from North Korea
30 November	Truman refers to possible use of atomic bomb
4–8 December	Truman/Attlee talks in Washington

1951

25 January	Cabinet agrees to vote against US resolution at UN condemning China as aggressor
26 January	Cabinet agrees to vote for compromise resolution
29 January	Cabinet agrees to increase rearmament programme to £4,700 million over three years
1 February	UN General Assembly condemns China as aggressor
15 March	Recapture of Seoul
11 April	Truman relieves MacArthur
23 April	Resignation of Aneurin Bevan over budget
15–24 June	UN forces consolidate positions beyond 38th parallel
10 July	Truce negotiations begin at Kaesong
23 August	Communists suspend armistice negotiations
11 September	Morrison/Acheson talks begin in United States. Gaitskell requests reduction in US rearmament demands
19 September	Attlee calls general election
25 October	Conservatives win election under Winston Churchill. Truce talks resume at Panmunjom
28 November	Anglo-American discussions of 'greater sanctions' statement

1952

3–23 January	Churchill and Eden visit United States
7 May	Truce talks deadlocked over 'voluntary repatriation' of POWs
8 May	Koje Uprising
22 May	British troops sent to Koje
12 June	Selwyn Lloyd and Lord Alexander hold talks with General Clark in Tokyo
23 June	US aircraft bomb power plant at Shuifeng Supung (Suiho). Protests in Britain
8 October	Americans suspend truce talks
14 October	UN General Assembly meets. Eden/Acheson disagreement over Indian peace plan
4 November	Republican candidate, Dwight D. Eisenhower, elected US President
3 December	UN General Assembly adopts modified Indian plan. Rejected by Beijing and Pyongyang

1953

3–9 January	Churchill visits United States. Talks with Eisenhower and Dulles
2 February	Eisenhower announces 7th Fleet will no longer 'neutralize' Taiwan. Eden criticizes this move in Parliament
5 March	Stalin dies
	Eden/Dulles talks in Washington
28 March	China and DPRK agree to exchange of sick and wounded POWs
26 April	Truce talks resume
7 May	Communists produce POW proposal. Britain protests at US response
11 May	Churchill proposes summit with new Russian leaders
25 May	US tables revised POW proposal at Panmunjom

4 June	China and DPRK agree with US proposal
18 June	Rhee releases North Korean POWs
20 June	Churchill suggests sponsoring coup against Rhee
27 July	Armistice signed
7 August	'Greater sanctions' warning issued

1954

22 January	Talks about a political conference on Korea collapse
26 April – 15 June	Geneva conference fails to reach agreement on Korean reunification

Further Reading

The special relationship and the cold war

There is an extensive literature on the British role in the early cold war. Particularly useful are: Terry Anderson, *The United States, Great Britain and the Cold War* (Columbia and London 1981); Robert M. Hathaway, *Ambiguous Partnership: Britain and America, 1944–1947* (New York 1981); and Fraser J. Harbutt, *The Iron Curtain: Churchill, America and the Origins of the Cold War* (New York 1986). Other books include: Donald Watt, *Succeeding John Bull: America in Britain's Place 1900–1975* (Cambridge 1984); Ritchie Ovendale (ed.), *The Foreign Policy of the British Labour Governments 1945–1951* (Leicester 1984); Ritchie Ovendale, *The English-Speaking Alliance: Britain, the United States, the Dominions and the Cold War 1945–51* (London 1985); Elisabeth Barker, *The British Between the Superpowers 1945–50* (London 1983); and Robin Edmonds, *Setting The Mould: The United States and Britain 1945–1950* (London 1986). The best account of the key role played by Ernest Bevin is Alan Bullock's *Ernest Bevin: Foreign Secretary 1945–1951* (London 1984). Defence relations are examined in John Baylis, *Anglo-American Defence Relations, 1939–1984: The Special Relationship* (London 1984). The atomic controversy is discussed in Margaret Gowing, *Independence and Deterrence: Britain and Atomic Energy 1945–1952* (2 vols, London 1974); and Timothy Botti, *The Long Wait: The Forging of the Anglo-American Nuclear Alliance, 1945–1948* (New York 1987). A brief summary of the literature can be found in David Dimbleby and David Reynolds, *An Ocean Apart: The Relationship between Britain and America in the Twentieth Century* (New York 1988).

The origins of the Korean War

The best account of origins of the war is Bruce Cumings' *The Origins of the Korean War* (Princeton 1981), which has influenced all subsequent studies. There are also useful interpretations in Bruce Cumings (ed.), *Child of Conflict: The Korean–American Relationship, 1943–1945* (Seattle 1983); and Frank Baldwin (ed.), *Without Parallel: The American–Korean Relationship Since 1945* (New York 1973). Excellent general surveys include Peter Lowe, *The Origins of the Korean War* (London 1986); and Bruce Cumings and Jon Halliday, *Korea: The Forgotten War* (London 1988), which is also a fresh and provocative study of the war itself.

Britain and the Korean War

Writing on the Korean War has been dominated by Americans. There is no comprehensive study of British policy, but several books on the conflict discuss Anglo-American relations. These include: Callum A. MacDonald, *Korea: The War Before Vietnam* (London 1986); Burton I. Kaufman, *The Korean War Challenges in Crisis, Credibility and Command* (New York 1986); Rosemary Foot, *The Wrong War: American Policy and the Dimensions of the Korean Conflict, 1950–1953* (Ithaca and London 1985); David Rees, *Korea: The Limited War* (London 1964); and James Cotton and Ian Neary (eds), *The Korean War in History* (Manchester 1989), a series of essays dealing largely with various aspects of British policy. Max Hastings, *The Korean War* (London 1987) is good on military operations but seriously flawed on the wider issues of diplomacy and strategy. American views on British policy can be found in: Dean G. Acheson, *Present at the Creation* (London 1970), an essential source; and Harry S. Truman, *Years of Trial and Hope* (New York 1956). Valuable perspectives on British policy and events at the UN can also be found in books about other countries that participated in the Korean War. Of particular value are: Denis Stairs, *The Diplomacy of Constraint: Canada, the Korean War and the United States* (Toronto

1975); and Robert O'Neill, *Australia in the Korean War* (2 vols, Canberra 1981). There is a discussion of Indian policy in Sarvepalli Gopal's *Jawaharlal Nehru*, vol. 2 (London 1979).

The books by Bullock, Barker and Ovendale cited above contain material on British policy during the early part of the war. An excellent overview of the impact of Korea on the Labour government is to be found in Kenneth O. Morgan, *Labour in Power 1945–1951* (London 1985). Kenneth Harris's *Attlee* (London 1982) exaggerates Attlee's achievement in Washington. Anthony Seldon's *Churchill's Indian Summer: The Conservative Government 1951–1955* (London 1981) is a comprehensive study. David Carlton's biography, *Anthony Eden* (London 1986) contains a definitive account of Eden's role. The relationship between the Conservative government and the Republican administration from the American perspective can be found in: Stephen E. Ambrose, *Eisenhower: The President 1952–1969* (New York 1984); Dwight D. Eisenhower, *Mandate for Change* (New York 1963); and Townsend Hoopes, *The Devil and John Foster Dulles* (London 1974). The political struggles over rearmament are refought in: Michael Foot, *Aneurin Bevan 1945–1960* (2 vols, London 1973); John Campbell, *Nye Bevan and the Mirage of British Socialism* (London 1987); and Philip M. Williams, *Hugh Gaitskell* (London 1982). British military operations are analysed in C. N. Barclay, *The First Commonwealth Division* (Aldershot 1954); and Jeffrey Grey, *The Commonwealth Armies and the Korean War* (Manchester 1988). A discussion of the press and the war can be found in Phillip Knightly, *The First Casualty* (London 1953).

Individual essays provide an essential addition to the fragmented general literature. Of particular interest are two papers in the International Studies Series edited by Ian Nish and produced by the International Centre for Economics and Related Disciplines, London School of Economics: Roger Dingman, 'Truman, Attlee and the Korean War Crisis', in *The East Asian Crisis, 1945–1951: The Problem of China, Korea and Japan*, International Studies Series 1982/1 (London 1982); and Roger Bullen, 'Great Britain, the United States and the Indian Armistice Resolution on the Korean War, November 1952', in

Aspects of Anglo-Korean Relations, International Studies Series 1984/1–2 (London 1984). Other important articles include: William Stueck, 'The Limits of Influence: British Policy and American Expansion of the War in Korea', *Pacific Historical Review*, vol. 55, 1986; Rosemary Foot, 'Anglo-American Relations in the Korean Crisis: The British Effort to Avert an Expanded War, December 1950 – January 1951', *Diplomatic History*, January 1986; Peter Lowe, 'Great Britain, Japan, and the Korean War, 1950–1951, *Proceedings of the British Association for Japanese Studies*, vol. 9, 1984; M.L. Dockrill, 'The Foreign Office, Anglo-American Relations and the Korean War, June 1950 – June 1951', *International Affairs*, 1986; Ra Jong-yil, 'Special Relationship at War: The Anglo-American Relationship during the Korean War', *Journal of Strategic Studies*, vol. 7, no. 3, September 1984; and Jon Halliday, 'Anti-Communism and the Korean War', in Ralph Miliband, John Saville and Marcel Liebman (eds), *Socialist Register 1984: The Uses of Anti-Communism* (London 1984)

The brutality of the war is captured in three books by British journalists: James Cameron, *Point of Departure* (London 1978); R.W. Thompson, *Cry Korea* (London 1951); and Rene Cutforth, *Korean Reporter* (London 1955). Also worthy of note is an account by a British soldier: Julian Tunstall's *I Fought in Korea* (London 1953) is a polemical piece. Eric Linklater's *Our Men in Korea* (London 1952) presents the official view. Memoirs by POWs include Anthony Farrar-Hockley, *The Edge of the Sword* (London 1954). The perspective from the other side can be found in the memoirs of the *Daily Worker* correspondent, Alan Winnington: *Breakfast with Mao: Memoirs of a Foreign Correspondent* (London 1986), and Hewlett Johnson, *Searching for the Light* (London, 1968). Contemporary accounts by British communists and those who sympathized with China and the DPRK include: Alan Winnington, *I Saw the Truth in Korea* (London 1950): Wilfred Burchett and Alan Winnington, *Koje Unscreened* (London 1953); Monica Felton, *What I Saw in Korea* (London 1952); and Hewlett Johnson (the 'Red Dean of Canterbury'), *I Appeal* (London 1952).

Index